# QUILTER'S WORKSHOP

## Joanie's
# Quilting Elements

## *7 Simple Steps to Navigate and Stitch*

## Joanie Zeier Poole

©2008 Joanie Zeier Poole

Published by

**kp krause publications**
*An Imprint of F+W Publications*

700 East State Street • Iola, WI 54990-0001
715-445-2214 • 888-457-2873
www.krausebooks.com

Our toll-free number to place an order or obtain
a free catalog is (800) 258-0929.

The following registered trademark terms and companies appear in this book:
American Folk and Fabric, Inc., Bernina®, Canson Tracing Paper™, Fabmore Cutlery™,
Ferd. Schmetz GmbH, Golden Threads™, Harriet's Treadle Arts, Hobbs Bonded Fibers®,
Mr. Scissors, Necchi Sewing Machines®, Olfa®, RJR Fabrics, Robert Kauffman Fabrics®,
Snips Free-Motion Slider™, Superior Threads, YLI Corporation®

Library of Congress Control Number: 2008926692

ISBN-13: 978-0-89689-650-5

ISBN-10: 0-89689-650-1


Designed by Donna Mummery

Edited by Barbara Smith, Jay Staten

Illustrated by Joanie Zeier Poole


Printed in China

# Acknowledgments

To you, my students and readers, I am grateful for the opportunity to share my experience and knowledge gained working on my quilts. For you to find value in my words makes my work worthwhile, and I thank you.

To all my family and friends who have shared in my enjoyment of this art, especially to Pam Levenhagen, for companionship as an artist.

To Aaron for expecting more of me, to Ben, who has stretched my world, and to Bob, my love and support, thank you all for providing the foundation for me to do the work I love.

To my parents, for teaching me self-reliance and the value of a good day's work, and for continuing to demonstrate generosity and productivity in your later years, Mom by hooking rugs for all of the family and Dad by making so many charity quilts.

# Contents

# Introduction

So you want to become a great machine quilter, but don't know where to begin. You may have already tried but were unhappy with the results. You may lack the confidence to stitch all over your nicely pieced top for fear of ruining it. Well, you have come to the right place. I have written this book to support you with solutions and to provide solid information broken down into simple steps. I encourage you to try, because if I can learn this, so can you!

I want you to look at machine quilting like a new adventure, one in which you can travel to places you have never been. You wouldn't start out on a journey without knowing where you were going or accumulating everything you need for the trip, so I have included all the essential information to prepare you for your expedition. All you need is this road map for success:

- Begin with a plan based on a solid design.

- Gather needed equipment.

- Learn the mind-body connection to imprint the travel plan in your brain.

- Practice to gain proficiency.

Free-motion quilting requires skills I developed over years of pushing myself beyond my comfort zone. All of my experience is available to you with this text. I have established a foundation of concepts and exercises to support you, opening a whole new world of free-motion to you. It will take some practice. Don't expect perfection on the first day. Enjoy the process and begin with realistic goals for progressing over time. I hope you will use this knowledge to experience the thrill of accomplishing quilting on the equipment you already own.

You will gain an understanding of how to stitch any designs you want, efficiently and with confidence. You will learn to examine the designs you have chosen and know where to steer the needle before you sit down at the machine, stressing the importance of the mind-body connection. I am excited to introduce my concepts of Continuous Outline and Continuous Object design designations, which offer you insight into how connected rows of elegant motifs are easily stitched.

My reason for writing this book is to encourage quilters of all skill levels, using any machine, to complete their own projects. I want them to have the satisfaction of creating three-dimensional treasures, uniquely their own. My intention is to provide seven simple steps, strategies for you to follow that will provide the needed information to avoid the pitfalls of machine quilting.

You will learn my in-depth thought process developed over years of practice, thoughts you may never have considered before that will alleviate tension in the stitching process. It would be impossible to pack all of this into one class, so, as in *Joanie's Design Elements*, I am inviting you into my workshop to share all of the valuable information that will make you a successful machine quilter. You can take these lessons from the comfort of your own home, working with your schedule, at a pace you can manage.

And so I have great expectations for you on our journey. Open your mind to new ideas and new knowledge, and if you follow the exercises, you will actively teach yourself the process and learn new skills that can greatly enhance your leisure time.

# How to Use This Book

This book is written from the perspective of a teacher, giving lessons just for you. Common questions are answered and concepts demonstrated in the seven steps. First, read the entire book. Assemble the suggested supplies to make your job easy. Next, learn how to navigate and stitch many quilting designs by following the exercises and helpful tips.

### How to Use the CD

I have included several original designs on the CD, which is in the back of this book. Like any copyrighted material, the designs are for your personal use only and are not to be used for commercial purposes nor copied for gifting, sharing or sales.

When you insert the CD-ROM into your computer, the menu may not appear on your screen automatically. For PC: To view the CD-ROM menu, click on the Start button on the lower-left corner of your screen. Select My Computer then double-click on CD, quilt design. Most computers will display the individual quilt design immediately when you double-click it. For MAC: To view the CD-ROM, double-click on desktop icon of CD. Designs will either open in Preview or Adobe Acrobat Reader. If your computer will not display the quilt designs, you may need to download a free computer program called Adobe Acrobat Reader, which is available for download at www.adobe.com.

To print the designs, choose one from the CD design page 127 and simply click on the identifying label from the CD. The designs will all print out on 8.5" x 11" paper. The project will print in four sections.

# A Note to Teachers and Designers

The author and the publisher invite you to consider teaching from this book. All materials are copyrighted, so please have appropriate respect for the author's intellectual property. For teachers, we advise that each student purchase a copy of the book containing the CD for use in the class. For further information and to use any part of this book or CD, please contact the author and publisher for permission.

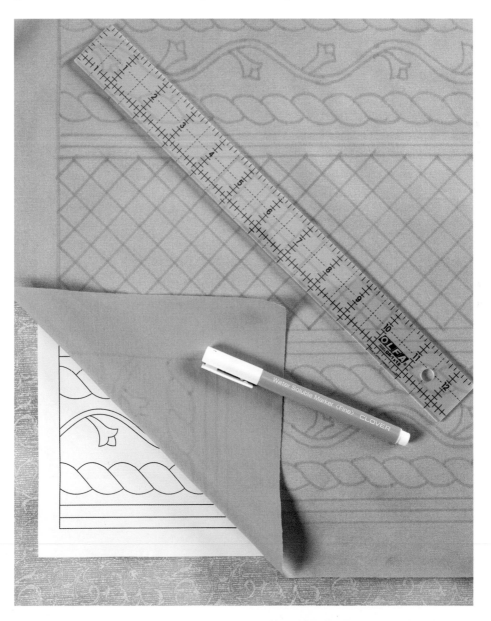

*Step One:*

# Freedom of the Open Road

We begin our journey with an explanation of just what free-motion quilting is, then we'll consider how the choice of machine impacts the work.

For free-motion quilting, all you really need is a sewing or quilting machine; you, the driver, will do the rest. Having a deeper understanding of the stitching process before you begin will put you at ease. Approach these instructions with a positive attitude and an open mind, and soon you will become a confident free-motion quilter. Even if some of my ideas are different from what you've heard in the past, please give them a try. I have spent eight years exploring supplies and developing this process in preparation for bringing this information to you.

OPPOSITE PAGE: *Quilted Evening Bag, 2004, Isabel Elements Stencil Packet from Golden Threads.*

## Just a Matter of Preference

Since my work has been done on a home machine and that is what I know best, the stitching information will be directed to quilting on a home machine, using refined free-motion techniques. If you are working on a larger machine, you will find much of the information useful; however, there will be times when you will need to adapt the procedures to the capabilities of your equipment.

# Understanding Free-motion Quilting

Free-motion quilting is a process for stitching the layers of a quilt together, using a sewing machine with the feed dogs lowered and a darning foot installed. Each design, whether drawn on the quilt top or held in the imagination of the quilter, is formed with a line of stitching that is guided by the movement of the quilt or machine. Without the feed dogs engaged to advance the fabric, the operator controls the stitch length and can steer the stitching in any direction, forming curvilinear or straight lines. Until you gain some experience, it may feel like driving on glare ice!

As long as the feed dogs can be lowered or covered, free-motion quilting can be performed on any machine, including long- and short-arm quilting machines, a frame that moves a domestic machine over a rolled quilt, or a domestic machine that is stationary. (The terms "home" and "domestic" can be interchanged, and they refer to a regular sewing machine.) Much of the information for stitching designs will be valuable regardless of the type of machine you choose to use.

Advanced free-motion techniques are needed for heirloom machine quilting, in which the scale of the work is refined. The use of smaller threads and needles allows for detailed and complex patterns. The intricate quilted designs produce three dimensions through the play of light and shadow over the quilt surface. Motifs appear brighter because the high areas catch the light, while low areas recede into the depth of the shadows.

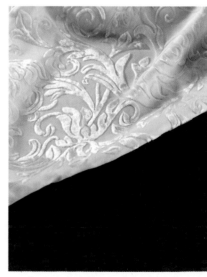

Look at the pattern of this scarf, from the Palace of Versailles in France. It is all one color, yet the contrast of the raised nap against the flat background provides the textured pattern.

# Home Machine Versus a Frame or Long-arm

When devising a plan for navigating and stitching quilting designs, there are important distinctions between using a long-arm or a home machine.

- First, long or short-arm machines are calibrated for commercial use and require larger needles and specific bobbins. They may not be able to handle the lightweight threads and fine needles needed to form tiny stitches for refined free-motion quilting, or they may require adjustments in the timing of the machine. Home machines require little or no adjustments when using fine thread.
- When a quilt sandwich is rolled on a frame, the stitching area is limited to a section of space across the width of the quilt, until it is rolled to expose another section. When a home machine is used, the stitching can occur anywhere on the quilt, unrestricted from top to bottom and from one edge to the other.

# My High Performing Low Riders

All of the projects photographed for this book, as well as my competition quilts (www. heirloomquiltingdesigns.com), were completed on home sewing machines that are from 45 years old to brand new. Success comes from the way I handle the machine with the feed dogs lowered and how I fill the surface with intricate designs.

When seeing my larger pieces, viewers sometime assume the quilts have been stitched on a long-arm machine, and they never consider that such quilting is possible on a home sewing machine. The key to using a home machine is how the quilt sandwich is maneuvered under the needle and how choosing the right supplies make the job much simpler. I am satisfied with the work accomplished with these machines and have no desire to change. The following factors impacted my decision to use a home machine:

- Space, or lack of it. I simply do not want to dedicate space in my home for a long-arm machine.
- Practicality. I already own several home sewing machines. (Who's counting?)
- Pattern selection. Some designs require maneuvering intricate motifs.
- Delicacy of the results. My stitches are tiny and the thread is very lightweight.
- Logistics. I teach on home sewing machines, which are light enough to lug to class!

For me, at this moment, the investment in a long-arm would be an expense I could not justify. I am able to stitch anything I want with the machines I already own, and I recently completed a piece 82" x 82", which is big enough for my requirements. My aspirations have never been geared toward making quilts to sell or to transform someone else's top into a quilt. I love to draw, write, teach, and create designs for you. However, I am also old enough and wise enough to never say never!

# Driving a Reliable Rig

And now we come to the question I am asked more than any other, which is "What machine do you have?" Some people have the misconception that, if only they had the same machine I use, they could do what I do. Well, here is a little bad news for them and the good news for you: It is the skill and attitude of the driver that makes a success. This skill can be learned with information and practice.

I learned free-motion quilting on reliable mechanical machines built in the mid 1960s, and I have won many awards for the quilts made on those machines. It is only recently that I've been stitching on new, high-end models. Imagine the challenge I had catching up on 45 years of technology! The only real disadvantage to those old girls is that, while they perform beautifully at high speeds for prolonged periods, the foot pedals get hot. I had my dealer make two extra pedals. Now I have two cooling while I am using the third.

As a teacher, it is advantageous for me to try as many machines as possible. Students bring all different brands and models to class, from the bright shiny new, to the beloved old faithful. We have had success free-motion quilting on antique Singer Featherweights, whose feed dogs can't be lowered, as well as a 25-year-old Necchi that didn't have a darning foot attachment. I suggested that the owner investigate adapting a foot from another machine. The result was a foot that not only functioned properly, it formed some of the nicest stitches in the entire classroom. The determination of the operator made her the success of the day.

Don't let an old machine hold you back from trying this work. If you own it, try it. What do you have to lose? Many of these machines have a lot of good years left in them.

A few of the sewing inventions offered in the past.

# Bells and Whistles

Having said that, there are wonderful new advancements, which help make our machine quilting go more smoothly. We need to keep our hands on the work while operating the machine. We need to know the quilt layers are secure when we stop stitching, for which the needle-stop-down feature is a real asset. A walking foot or even-feed feature is advantageous for anchoring the quilt, holding the many layers securely for quilting and for adding binding. Here are a few more performance enhancers that aid in free-motion quilting:

- The ability to lower the feed dogs.
- The capacity to make tension adjustments for wonderfully formed stitches, when using lightweight and invisible thread.
- Adjustable presser-foot pressure.
- A longer machine head makes it easier to fit a quilt in a tight space.

Because I learned this skill on old machines without bells and whistles, I actually feel I have more freedom without the gadgets. I have learned to have better control of the foot pedal to start and stop stitching without the machine deciding when to take a stitch. I can stitch in any direction, and I'm not limited in turning the quilt because it is attached to rollers or a fabric-moving device. I have an open field of vision, not restricted by a large foot. But I also know some very experienced garment sewers who just were not getting free-motion quilting. They purchased a gizmo to regulate stitch length, and with it, they are happily and successfully completing their projects. That is fine, if you can afford the investment. Do whatever it takes.

# Finding a Reliable Pit Crew

You are asking your machine to do things it was not calibrated for at the factory, so you will need to learn how to adjust it. Establish a relationship with a dealer and study your owner's manual. If you don't have a dealer in your area, look on the Internet or talk to dealers at a quilt show to get advice for free-motion quilting with your machine. The educational opportunities and service record of your local dealer are important factors in choosing a machine. You can find that information by asking other sewers about the reliability of their service people.

Now that you know what to look for, if you are in the market for a new machine, watch out for sticker shock and keep in mind, you get what you pay for. Purchase the best you can afford. In some cases that might mean choosing a good used machine. I advised my nieces, who cannot afford a major investment at this time of their lives, to consider a good quality older machine with more features for the same dollars as a new, inexpensive starter machine. There may be many good years left in a machine that someone else traded in, not because she was unhappy. On the contrary, she may have loved the machine and just wanted to upgrade to more features.

Again, this all goes back to reliable service. The guys on the bench at my local shop can fix anything on my good old machines, and the educators there give great advice from their vast experience and training. When you do buy any new-to-you machine, for goodness sake, make the time to attend the new-owner classes offered for both new and used machines. Learn all you can about what your machine can do for you.

# Mental Fortitude Is Not a Mental Illness

I am a dreamer and a believer in "Where there is a will there is a way." I preach that desire is the strongest factor in learning anything. Free-motion quilting may feel foreign to you at first. Even if you have stitched all your life, lowering the feed dogs adds an entirely new dimension to the experience.

If you met me at a show or attended one of my lectures, you may have heard me say this before, it's only fabric, so what are you afraid of? What do you have to lose? I am sure you have plenty of fabric to spare. So I suggest, isn't there the possibility that learning this skill will be a life-altering challenge that could elevate your quilting experience and enable you to complete your own quilts on a machine you already own?

We all need to practice until we find the key to unlock that little place in the brain that holds us back. Compare the risk of trying free-motion quilting, and learning from your mistakes, to the potential for learning something that could change your life. Maybe you will do better than you thought you would. The only way to fail at this is never to have tried!

Everything you have done in your quilting life until today is practice for what you are about to learn. Embrace that knowledge and experience, blend it with the concepts offered in this book. Put this new information to good use everyday if you use your home machine, have a long-arm, or use a frame. I applaud your commitment to this industry, for fun or career. My advice is relevant no matter what machine or attachments you try, but you need to know where you are going to successfully stitch with any machine, so let's discuss that in Step Two.

*OPPOSITE PAGE: Geneva Quilt, 2007, Options Stencil from Golden Threads*

*Step Two:*

# Charting Rugged Terrain

Just how do you expect to get anywhere if you don't know where to go? When planning any journey, we must consider the best route to avoid unnecessary interruptions in our trip. When traveling by car, we begin by studying the state highways that take us to a city, and then a street map to negotiate to our final destination. When our ultimate objective is to quilt by machine, we must be able to read the quilt layout like a map, plotting out where to begin and end each segment of the journey. Your mission will be much more successful when you study the terrain and plan a customized route for each quilt before you begin.

OPPOSITE PAGE: *Classic Tiles Table Mat from Elegant Machine Quilting (KP Books, 2005).*

# Rules of the Road

My husband's grandfather, William "Homer" Arneson, always used to say, "You better look where you're driving or drive where you're looking!" His simple wisdom was lost on his wife, Emma, who thought that the yellow line meant it was a good time to pass, and a double yellow line meant twice as good!

Whether you are free-motion quilting or pursuing any new endeavor in life, a well-thought-out plan of action is beneficial. When sewing a patchwork seam, you don't need to think about where to steer the needle or how many times to begin a new thread; you just know where to stitch. But with free-motion quilting, you are essentially drawing or tracing design outlines with your sewing machine. Understanding how to begin and end each thread, where to anchor the layers, and how to complete the motifs with the fewest starts and stops is critical to the success of your work.

After teaching machine quilting for several years, I began noticing many analogies to driving a car. Much of the advice given to kids when they learn to drive can apply to learning free-motion quilting:

- Study the map before you take off, to know where you are going.
- Don't stare at the hood ornament; look ahead down the road.
- Slow down and proceed with caution when encountering a curve or busy intersection.
- There will be penalties for speeding and for making U-turns in unauthorized areas.
- If you intend to stop, remember to take your foot off the gas.
- Don't drive if you have had too much to drink.

This is all good advice to relieve stress when practicing, to build confidence and gain experience, for anyone getting behind the wheel in traffic or trying free-motion quilting for the first time. So we can begin our machine-quilting journey by understanding our entire route before we put the vehicle in gear.

Single Initial Pincushion from Fancy Alphabet Pattern

# Plotting Your Own Road Map

Our first task is to divide and conquer the space. We want to establish work zones, sections to work within, beginning at the center of the quilt and progressing outward. Later, we will fill in the motifs, grids, and background fillers.

Let's assume we have a top that is marked and pin basted. Even though the quilt sandwich is held together with pins, large areas of the top must be sectioned off before smaller details can be added. This is accomplished by anchoring the layers with a line of stitching along patchwork or around objects, progressing from the center outward. Keep the distribution of stitching as equal as possible across the quilt surface throughout the quilting process.

# Stitching Sequence

Here is the logical order to follow when machine quilting any layout. We will discuss securing each thread in Step Five.

*1* Stabilize the layers by stitching the longest lines of the design or by stitching along the patchwork and border seams first.

*2* After the quilt has been anchored into sections, check the back for any puckering. If you need to tear out stitching, this is the time to do it.

*3* Next, follow the outlines of the motifs.

*4* Stitch the background grids.

*5* Fill in the details of the motifs.

*6* Complete the quilting by filling the background around the motifs.

# Stabilizing the Layers

When quilting a patchwork top, you may want to simply follow along the seams of the blocks to stabilize the layers. But, if you are quilting a medallion-style appliqué pattern or a wholecloth layout, your journey may be less predictable. Follow whatever outlines are available to hold the layers together, beginning with the centermost outline and progressing outward.

Remember, each time you move to a new area, you must secure the new thread, stitch the line, and end it with locking stitches just past the place where the stitching began.

For this example, follow this navigation guide used for the Ivy Curl Quilt layout. Don't worry that this is a lot to get all at once. Each of these operations will be covered again later.

---

*1* Secure your thread and stitch the outline of the oval.

*2* Next, stitch in the ditch of both edges of the inner border.

*3* Then stitch in the ditch of the outer border.

*4* Run a line of basting stitches around the outside edge of the quilt to hold the layers together.

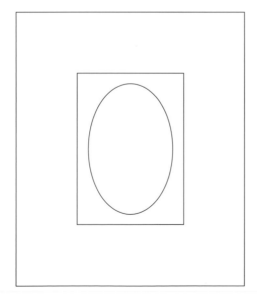

*5* Stitch the motifs, starting from the center. The designs touch, so they are all connected into groups that are stitched with one thread.

*6* Fill in the grid and quilt around the large-scale designs on the floral fabric.

*7* If stippling is desired around our ivy motifs, add it last.

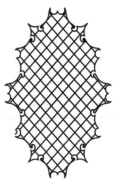

OPPOSITE PAGE: *Ivy Curl Quilt, 2007*

# Taking a Test Drive

Put on your glasses as we examine the details of our next trip, mapping one individual motif. Understanding where to place the needle and how to direct the line of stitching around the motif is important. Know in advance where to stop and start a new thread, so you don't have to make that decision while the machine is running. Planning your starts and stops will allow you to concentrate on following the line accurately.

With the top divided into secure sections, direct your focus to the details of the quilting designs. Concentrate your stitching in a small area by smoothing about a 12" space to work within. This is the only section of the quilt you will be moving. Support the rest of the quilt on all sides. Any portion falling off the table will cause tension, which will distort the stitches.

# Making the Mind-Body Connection

For this demonstration, we will use the Classic Tiles Square design from the tablemat, coasters, and pincushion in the photo. There is a strong connection between tracing a design with a marking tool, or your finger, and following the marked design outline with a needle when stitching. Take the time to carefully map out a path for each quilting motif and practice tracing around the entire design to familiarize yourself with its shapes. Are you noticing the repeated segments of the design (loops, scallops, circles)?

Classic Tiles projects from *Elegant Machine Quilting*, (KP Books, 20050)

# Traveling the Design

By first understanding the shape that is to be stitched then adding a stitching rhythm to like segments of that shape, your stitch length will be more consistent. A rhythm can be established by counting the time it takes to complete one segment of the design. For example, three counts to go up one side of the loop, three counts to come down the other side.

Let's put our theory into practice with this exercise:

*1* Print the Classic Tile Square quilting design from the CD.

*2* Follow the outline with your finger, creating a road map to follow in your head.

*3* Add a rhythm. In areas of like distances, count out beats to stitch at the same rate of speed each time that segment of the design is encountered.

*4* Unthread your machine and guide it over the shapes of the design, stitching through the paper. Just try to stay on the lines. Practice this over and over until you are comfortable guiding the needle to follow the shapes.

With a solid plan of action, you will avoid getting hung up on achieving a perfect stitch length before you know where to drive.

# Negotiating Curves

Tracing with your finger and following the road map in your head, you will naturally slow down when you come to a sharp curve in the design or when you need to retrace a line of stitching. Retracing is like driving a car into a parking space then backing out of it. Slow down. Vary the speed of the machine depending on the difficulty of the design. Stitch at a speed you are comfortable with to stay on the lines, even if it's slow. This is not a race.

## Setting Cruise Control

You may have a speed setting on your machine. If the machine feels like it is stitching too fast for you to control, set it to a slower speed.

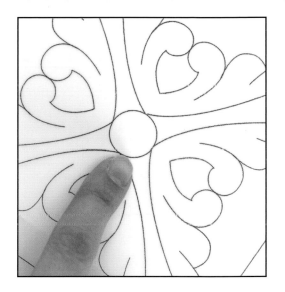

Here's a place on a design where you may want to slow the speed of the machine down.

# Do a Test Lap

With this exercise, you will become comfortable with handling the quilt bundle, learn to use your large-motor skills and discover a freedom to stitch anywhere. Purchase a yard of fabric with a large-scale floral or baby print. Layer and pin-baste the fabric, batting and backing. Load your machine with invisible or lightweight thread and set it up for free-motion quilting.

Begin stitching in the center of the piece and work toward the outer edges, following the pattern on the fabric. Stitch one motif and drive right on to the next without stopping. Don't worry about being perfect, you won't see the individual stitches. Let go, be free and just do it! When you are comfortable with a big pattern, try a smaller design and before you know it you will be ready for micro stippling.

# Driving in the Dark

If, in the past, you were nervous about ruining your nicely pieced top with free-motion quilting, you probably hadn't studied the layout, nor understood how to handle the quilt bundle before you began stitching the top. That was just too much to do and think about all at once with the machine running! Now you know where to begin and how to divide the quilt into manageable sections. And best of all, you have discovered the benefits of the mind-body connection.

*OPPOSITE PAGE: Hand-quilted Sailboats at Sea pattern, 1985.*

*Step Three:*

# Makes and Models of Designs

One of the most important goals in machine quilting is to become adept at connecting motifs without interrupting the line of stitching. This eliminates the need to begin and end new threads and saves time. Learning which designs can be used with background fillers is another valuable lesson. To aid you in these tasks, I am introducing the concept of dividing designs into three well-defined categories: continuous line, continuous outline and continuous object designs. I will then offer insight to my approach for stitching these designs. Once you understand why the distinctions are important, your machine quilting life will become much less stressful.

In this step we will closely examine quilting designs used either singly or joined into groups or rows. Of all the information presented in this book, I am most excited to share this with you. I believe it will immediately increase your level of success and enjoyment in machine quilting.

OPPOSITE PAGE: *Huron Quilts, 2007, printable designs on CD.*

# Line Art or Closed Object

Before we get to stitching groups of motifs, we need to take one little side trip. Let's take a minute to contemplate stitching individual objects, not continuous patterns. We need to determine if the object is line art or a closed shape to know whether it can be used with background fillers.

First, let's begin with a basic comparison. The following illustration shows what appears to be a leaf. You can stitch completely around the leaf and return to the starting place with one thread, but the object outline is open at the stem end.

If a background filler is desired with this leaf, adjustments will need to be made to the design. By adding to the outline, a closed object can be created. It can still be stitched with one thread, but now that we have closed the gap, a filler pattern can be used around the leaf.

An individual leaf is used to demonstrate a continuous route that connects objects scattered about the top, not touching one another. In this case, simply stitch one leaf and then sew a drunkard's path of stippling to the next one.

After all of the motifs have been stitched, fill in the entire background with stippling.

In contrast to the simplicity of these leaves, the Eiffel Tower is also a closed object, albeit a complicated one. The path of its outline can be followed with a single thread and details added after it is complete. With a design this intricate, the scale of the background filler must be tiny to contrast the object. The use of colored thread also helps to distinguish the fine lines of the structure from the stippling.

Detail from *Fais de beaux rêves!*, 2005.

# Categories of Design

Let's consider using designs joined into groups and rows. First, we will learn to recognize what we're looking at and then apply solutions for navigating those situations.

The quilting designs included here have a distinctive look of elegance and sophistication, designed to excite you with a fresh approach to filling the plain areas of your quilts. The stylized shapes I created have enough volume to stand out from the background fillers and recreate the play of light and shadow across the surface of a quilt, like carvings in art and architecture. While these designs look complicated, they can be easily stitched by machine.

I developed a strategy for stitching each design to fill borders and blocks. Studying the paths created by the outlines of connected motifs revealed that the designs could be placed in categories with similar quilting instructions.

Continuous line designs are fine, but I want designs with intricate shapes that stand out when the background is filled. Continuous outline and continuous object designs are new design categories, my own terminology for these basic groups of designs. Through my teaching experience, I understand how helpful this information is. With these lessons you will be able to look at a design, determine its category and apply the stitching advice. How clever, understanding how to navigate a design before you begin to stitch. Where have you heard that before?

## Category 1. Continuous-line designs

Continuous-line designs are available for machine quilters who want to eliminate the need to begin and end new threads frequently. Most continuous-line designs are just that, uninterrupted lines of stitching. Some of the designs look like objects. Others are decorative lines made up of curves, which can be stitched with a single line traveling across the width of the quilt. For borders, these designs turn at the corners and go all around the quilt. Designs of this type are available as books, design packets, stencils, or pantographs, which are patterns printed on long rolls of paper.

Continuous-line designs are sought after by machine quilters because they are so quick to stitch. They are especially attractive to long-arm quilters or those who use a frame, because when the quilt is attached to rollers, the stitching area is constrained to a strip across the quilt. These designs can be followed with one thread across the quilt, and multiple rows of these designs quickly fill space.

Some patterns may give the appearance of leaves or roses, but when closely examined, they are not closed objects at all, just continuous lines. The following leaf design appears to be an object, but look closely, the stem outlines don't meet. The importance of this distinction will become clear as we continue this lesson.

# Delectable Mountain Trek

Delectable Mountain Quilt, 1997. Hooked rug, Margaret Walsh Zeier.

Let's follow the progression of quilting a patchwork Delectable Mountain quilt top, using this simple continuous line design I created years before learning free-motion quilting. For this quilt, I used my home machine with the walking foot attached and the feed dogs engaged. Each time I encountered a turn in the pattern, I had to pivot the quilt sandwich to stitch in a different direction.

*1* Begin by anchoring the layers with stitch-in-the-ditch quilting along the blocks and borders. Remember to check the back for any puckers before continuing.

*2* Add details to each pieced block, following the seam lines of the patchwork.

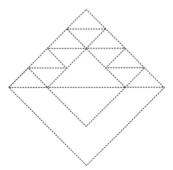

The quilt is now anchored well enough that we should not encounter any problems while adding details anywhere on the top. One continuous line of stitching will complete the designs in the plain blocks and all of the setting triangles.

*3* Secure a thread where indicated by the arrow in the following illustration. Drive on the marked line up to the corner and across the top row of half designs, filling the setting triangles.

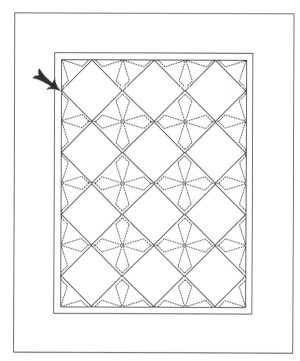

*4* Turn the corner, drive down to the top row of blocks. Stitch the top half of the designs across the row, but do not stitch inside the setting triangle on the left. Instead, turn and stitch the bottom half of the designs back across to the setting triangle on the right.

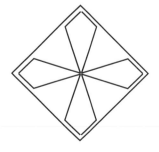

*5* Next, travel down to the lower row, and continue in this manner, working downward.

*6* When you reach the bottom, stitch across the setting triangles, turn the corner and travel up the triangles, returning to the place you began. Cross over the first stitches and secure the thread. Wow! Talk about your continuous-line design!

Since no stippling was intended, this continuous-line pattern was a good choice for this utilitarian quilt.

## Category 2. Continuous-outline designs

Continuous-outline designs, for the most part, require two parallel lines of stitching that flow from one end of a space to the other or completely around a border. The designs are comprised of a double outline, which forms a channel of puffy space between two stitched lines, and may have motifs such as leaves or flowers attached.

As we have already established, when machine quilting, we are generally working from the center of the quilt outward, so when I refer to the inner line, I mean the one closest to the quilt center, and the outer line is the farthest one from the center.

Now, look at the following single-line design. This vine with leaves has one continuous line of stitching.

By adding a second outline to the vine, we give it volume, making a puffy channel of unquilted space between the lines. Now background fillers can be used with this leaf design.

If a continuous-outline design is intended to be used with a background filler, it needs to puff up when the background is flattened. That channel of space between the two parallel lines must be wider than the scale of the filler to distinguish it from the background. Even if a narrow vine is used, the puffy area must be larger than the scale of the stippling.

## Fixing mistakes

If you strayed off the marked line when stitching row 1 of the vine, use your stitching line as a guide for sewing row 2, spacing the second line equidistant from the first. Your mistake will be less noticeable and it will look better to have both rows that match when the marked line is washed away.

The simple flower vine in the next illustration is a continuous-outline design. There are two parallel lines with buds attached. Let me explain how simple it will be for you to stitch this design for a project like the neck-roll pillow pattern on page 100.

Stitching a continuous-outline design is quite simple when you understand that it requires two lines of stitching to complete the design. First, stitch row 1 across the length of the marked design, adding the buds as you go. (The tip of the bud requires a bit of retracing.) Next, stitch row 2 either by sewing in the opposite direction (no need to cut the thread) or by cutting the thread and beginning again at the starting place for row 1.

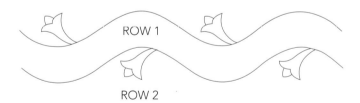

ROW 1

ROW 2

This Greek Key design (on the CD, file Greek Key) is a continuous-outline design requiring two lines of stitching to complete. Micro stippling could be used to fill the spaces around the design if desired.

## Category 3. Continuous-object designs

The designs used for the first two categories make good examples for demonstrating the driving path, but they are a bit ordinary. Let's have some real fun! Continuous-object designs are constructed as closed objects with interesting outlines. These motifs are puffy, having greater volume than the channels of the continuous-outline patterns. They can be used with fillers that flatten the background around them. For designers, that extra volume affords space to create attention-grabbing designs that sometimes have very intriguing paths to follow. But, with the navigation solutions you have already learned, a complicated outline won't concern you. After all, there is a marked line to follow, and you are equipped to plan the stitching route.

When your layout calls for closed objects that are connected into groups or used in rows with the motifs touching, the method for stitching is similar to continuous-outline designs, in that the design has multiple lines of stitching. That spot where the motifs touch creates a place where the designs can be divided and stitched with two or more continuous lines of stitching.

First, learn to follow the outline to stitch a single motif then plan a stitching route when using multiple designs. A motif can be as simple as a shamrock or as complicated as the Eiffel Tower.

Begin stitching the individual motif by securing a thread along the base. Travel around the entire outline and return to where you started. End the thread by securing it with a few stitches beyond the starting point.

In the following illustration, we see a row of shamrocks that do not touch one another but rest on the seam line of a border. (The printable design is on the CD, file Shamrock). To use one thread to connect this row of motifs, simply stitch one complete design then follow the border seam to pass to the next motif.

# Continuous Outline or Continuous Object?

For some designs, it's not quite so easy to distinguish which category they fall into. Is it continuous outline or continuous object? Now that you know how to stitch both, it really does not matter which category it is in. The categories are just teaching tools. My point is you are now trained to look at any design and plan a solution for easy stitching. If you encounter a design that looks like it could be in either category, it won't matter because you know how to deal with both. Here is a good example. Are there two parallel rows of stitching in the following illustration, or are these little objects that are touching?

This rope design has been used for years by hand quilters, who can easily slip their needle between layers and begin stitching anywhere on the design they want. Machine quilters must take a new approach to navigate this design. Look at the design as having two lines of stitching, one that is made of simple scallops, and one with scallops having an extended line that is retraced in order to travel on to the next.

Now that you understand how to stitch the rope designs, try lengthening the lines to fill a wider space.

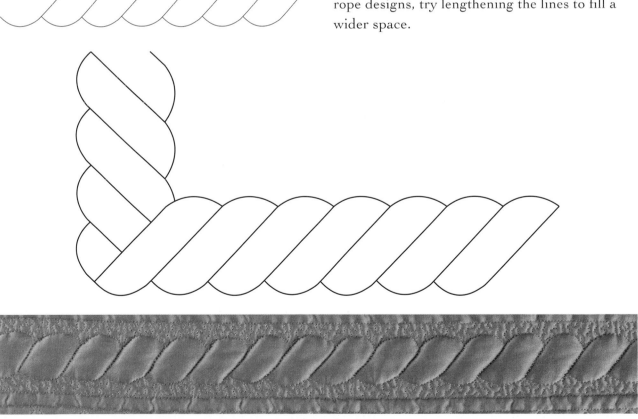

# Traveling the Huron Highway

The elegant new single motif, called Huron, was designed especially for you, to provide an example of the many ways a continuous object design can be used in a layout (printable designs are on the CD, file Huron 1). It has some delicate curves that will make it interesting to play with. Follow the stitching line with your finger to see how this single motif can be completed with one line of stitching. Use the following steps to stitch the design:

*1* Secure a thread at the base of the design.

*2* Stitch the outside line all the way around to the bottom of the opposite side.

*3* Continue stitching up and then back down the inside line until you pass the starting point and secure your stitches.

*OPPOSITE PAGE: Huron Quilts, 2007, printable designs on CD.*

Now, imagine using the Huron design between the seam lines of a border. We can use the same plan for stitching this row of motifs that we used for the shamrocks resting on a line; that is, use the seam line as a road to travel to the next motif.

The same process applies when the motif is flipped to make an alternate design. You can still travel from one motif to the next on the line and complete each motif as an individual closed object, stitching as many motifs as needed with one thread.

Our travel plans need to change, however, when the motifs are arranged into pairs, squares, and wreaths, or when they are used to fill a border. When our layout calls for continuous rows of closed objects, we no longer want to stitch each one as an individual motif. Our goal is to stitch a continuous group of objects, using one thread.

When we use the motif as a pair with bases touching, the design can be stitched with one thread, as follows:

*1* Begin by securing the thread where the two bases touch.

*2* Follow the outline all the way around both designs.

*3* Next, travel the line inside both designs.

*4* Return to the starting place and retrace over the top of the first secured stitches.

Now consider the stitching path when the designs touch, side by side, and are placed in a row for a border. When closed objects touch, we have the opportunity to divide the design into a top half and a bottom half.

View the border as one unit having an inside path and an outside path on which you can travel from one motif to the next. Stitch half of the design on the first trip and complete the rest of the design on the second pass: follow line 1 across the entire quilt to the end of the row and continue stitching line 2 to complete the second half of the design with the same thread. For a border, follow the inner line around the whole quilt then stitch the outer line.

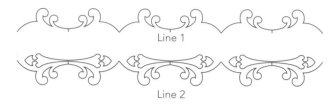

Line 1

Line 2

In the following illustration, the pairs of Huron motifs are resting on a line. It may be just a marked and stitched line, or it could be the seam line of two different fabrics. Remember our example with the shamrock. The line is used as a highway to travel to the place where the next motifs are touching the line.

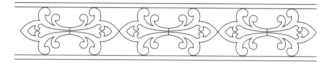

The same concept applies when the rows are standing upright, although a border of facing pairs of motifs could be approached in several ways. Follow the outline with your finger to find a path completing a pair and moving on to the next. You could stitch them as one motif pair attached to one seam line or as two rows of motifs attached to two different seam lines. Consider each method and decide which one is easier for you. Either process will require several passes across the quilt to complete the rows.

The same criteria will direct you to decide how to stitch the following alternate design.

When four of the pretty motifs are used to form a block design and their outlines touch, they can be stitched as continuous-object designs. A circle was added to the center of the square to connect the motifs and to direct the flow of traffic from one motif to the next.

*1* Begin by securing a thread on the circle.

*2* Stitch the inner line of each motif, moving from one to the next on the circle.

*3* Next, stitch the outer lines of each motif, then secure the thread.

Here's the icing on the cake! Eight motifs can be arranged into a continuous-object wreath. Having this concept to rely on when you use any motif will expand the use of designs you may already own.

To sew the wreath, split the design into two lines of stitching.

# Divide and Conquer

Classic tiles border design

Here is a sophisticated border design. Before you read this book, you might have looked at it and thought that the individual motifs would be difficult to stitch by machine. But you now know that, when the motifs touch one another, they can easily be stitched as a continuous-object design.

Look at the stitching guide indicating the design is divided where the motifs touch. We have an inner line and an outer line to stitch on. Sections of the outer line need to be re-traced, but it is stitched with one continuous piece of thread.

*1* Begin at the bottom intersection of two motifs. Travel around the entire square on the inner line, retracing where necessary, back to the beginning point.

*2* Continue on the outer line with the same thread.

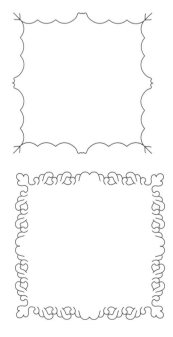

The following leaf design, used as a border for the table runner, is stitched with two separate lines, requiring two pieces of thread.

The first stitching is a simple line of scallops, and the second line of stitching includes the entire outline and all of the inner veins.

Autumn leaf table runner from *Elegant Machine Quilting*, (KP Books, 2005)

# On the Road

Don't let the importance of what you just learned be lost in the simplicity. With the understanding of the three design categories and the stitching advice in the rest of this book, you may no longer be satisfied to use the designs as they are. That closet full of stencil designs you thought you would never use again because they were purchased for hand quilting, may be easily stitched by machine with one continuous thread. If you already own books or packets full of continuous-line designs, get them out and use them.

Now that you have the knowledge to navigate complicated designs, single motifs can pull double duty filling borders and blocks. Challenge your quilting ability be using the motifs to create your own designs.

*Step Four:*

# Revving Up for the Long Haul

In my classes, I stress that students consider the end use of each quilt before they begin the process of choosing fabric, a pattern, and construction techniques for the project. What is the purpose of this journey? Is your destination the industrial park or the art museum? Knowing the life expectancy of the project will clarify the materials and processes used to construct it. Consider the extent of the quilting necessary, which will determine the time spent stitching. I encourage you to have a realistic outcome for your piece before you invest in materials.

This lesson covers the equipment and supplies used for re-fined free-motion quilting. I have included my favorites, which will help create success, and the reasons I chose them. If you are making display-only pieces, these materials should work well for you, too. If your intention is to construct utilitarian quilts, do some research on heavy-duty materials. The stitching concepts, however, will be beneficial to any machine quilter, and they will be adaptable to any outcome.

*OPPOSITE PAGE: Radiant Elements Quilt by author and a Charity Quilt by Norbert Zeier.*

# Fill Up with Premium

Whether you are new to quilting or have used the same products many times, try experimenting with different threads, batting, and fabrics. Familiarize yourself with how different products function. I recommend purchasing the best quality tools and supplies you can afford. You will be investing many hours on a project, and the job will go more smoothly if you use good materials. Be sure to keep your equipment in good working order, too.

# Pre-washing

Pre-washing fabrics will not only preshrink them, but it will also test for colorfastness. Since most of the marking I do is with a water-soluble marker, I want the security of knowing that no bleeding will occur when the piece is submerged in water to remove the marks.

- Wash each fabric alone in a white sink to check for dye bleeding.
- If bleeding persists, either don't use that fabric or treat it with a product that will set the color permanently.
- Partially dry each piece in a clothes dryer, then press completely dry.

# Pressing

When machine quilting, avoid any interruption in the stitching rhythm that causes uneven stitching. If the layout includes patchwork, a pressing plan is necessary for each block seam, as well as for assembling the entire top. Construct flat, accurately pieced tops that are free of bumps by pressing seam allowances open when practical, which equalizes the thickness of the layers.

Use spray starch to stabilize the fabric and increase accuracy before you cut patches for patchwork or appliqué blocks and for long border strips. To avoid flaking, spray the fabric then let the starch penetrate the fabric a few minutes before pressing.

Noah's Ark Hooked Rug, Margaret Walsh Zeier.

# Marking

Patterns and motifs intended to be stitched with free-motion techniques are usually drawn on the quilt top with water-soluble pencils or markers. Some background patterns, such as grids, are marked, while others, including stippling, are imprinted in your brain.

In the past, marking may have seemed like a tedious chore. Contemplate this: tracing the design numerous times will help you understand how to navigate it for stitching. You are performing a necessary task, and as an added bonus, you are gaining valuable training for stitching the design by imprinting the stitching path in your brain.

I know that when I draw my own designs from scratch, I can easily navigate them with a sewing machine because my brain has already figured out how the parts connect. If you draw it, you can stitch it. We will cover this further in Step Six.

There are many marking tools available. Whatever you choose, use a light touch. The less you put on, the less you have to take off. Water-soluble markers are available in blue for light colors or as white pencils for dark fabrics. Test any marker on each fabric before using it.

There are times when I stitch designs that have been marked or printed on paper. I use lightweight quilting paper by Golden Threads if I mark by hand, or Canson tracing paper if the design is generated from my computer and printer. After tracing or printing the design onto the paper, it is pinned in place on the quilt. I stitch the design, then gently remove the paper.

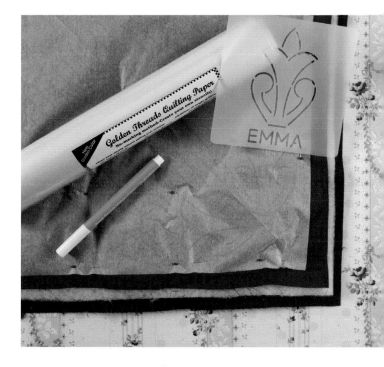

## Removing Markings

To remove the markings, submerge the entire piece in cold water until the lines are completely gone, then lay the quilt flat to dry. If blocking is needed, gently persuade the quilt into shape with your hands and tape it down, if necessary.

## Don't repeat my mistake!

I recommend that you do not remove any of the water-soluble markings until all of the quilting has been completed. I once was so anxious to get a peek at my stitching that I removed the marks by spritzing the marked outlines with water before I filled the background with stippling. The result was uneven shrinkage and the tedious job of flattening the background so I could stipple it without puckers.

# Batting

In my experience, Hobb's Heirloom or Tuscany Wool compresses nicely to fit under the machine and then springs back. It is 100 percent wool, completely washable, and it resists bearding. This batting is lightweight, which makes it a delight when handling a large quilt.

With any batting, plan for some shrinkage from washing, and the more quilting you do, the smaller your quilt will become.

## Preparing Batting

When possible, open the package of batting and let it rest overnight to relax the fibers, or just toss the batting in the clothes dryer to eliminate wrinkles.

# Basting

Machine quilters baste the layers of their quilts with safety pins rather than thread, to avoid getting the presser foot caught in the basting stitches during the quilting process. I use tiny, gold safety pins in sizes 0003 and 0004. The pins are inexpensive, and they don't get in the way while I am quilting. The thin, soft metal makes them easy to close and leaves only tiny holes in the fabric. They also add less weight to the quilt sandwich.

Fine straight pins can also be used for temporarily holding the layers of small projects together for quilting or for holding the pattern in place when quilting through paper. Here is a quick overview for basting a small project:

*1* Choose a hard work surface that is at a comfortable height for you to stand and work, such as a kitchen counter.

*2* Use masking tape to secure the backing fabric to the counter, wrong side up. Avoid stretching the layers when basting, because this will cause puckering during quilting.

*3* Smooth the batting on top of the backing.

*4* Center the top layer, right side up, over the first two layers and use tape to hold it down securely.

*5* Pin-baste with small pins. Start from the center and work outward, placing pins every 4" to 5". Avoid the quilting pattern lines whenever possible.

*6* Gently remove the tape from all of the layers, using caution so that the fabric edge does not ravel.

# Setting Up Your Workspace

Set up your sewing area to avoid aches and pains. A table height of about 30" off the floor should allow your elbows to bend at a 90-degree angle. To achieve a consistent stitch length, the area must be large enough to support the weight of the quilt, so it doesn't hang off the edges and pull the thread, which would distort the stitches.

Use an office chair with good back support and adjustable height. Sit with your body directly in front of the needle. Sitting off center may cause stress on your back, and it will distort your view of the work.

Three-in-one extension table

## Extending the work surface

Since I have several machines and travel often to work and teach, I use an add-on table that adapts to any machine. It is a portable extension table, a storage container for accessories, and a light box all in one item. I love it!

# Check the Headlights

Proper lighting is important when following intricate pattern lines, especially those marked on dark fabric. Here are a few suggestions:

- Be sure your eyeglass prescription is accurate for detailed work.
- Try directing whatever lighting you are using at different angles to determine which works best. Switch off the machine's light to see if that will help you to see the pattern lines better.

- Stop stitching every half hour, get up, and walk around. Look out the window at something in the distance to give your eyes a break from the strain of close-up work.
- Use eye drops to soothe your eyes when you sew for prolonged periods of time.
- Consider using a magnifying lens that is surrounded by a ring of fluorescent light. It is placed in a floor stand either next to or behind the worktable.

# Why Two Spool Pins?

Here is some advice from thread expert Heather Purcell of Superior Threads:

It's amazing how placing the spool on your machine the way the thread was intended to be unwound will solve problems such as breakage, uneven stitches, and improper thread tension. Spools are available in two styles, cross-wound and straight-wound, also referred to as stacked. Sewing machines usually come with two separate spool pins, with the vertical spool pin on the top and the horizontal spool pin that lays flat at the front of the machine.

The cross-wound spools (often long and narrow) are intended for use with the horizontal spool pin. They are designed so that the thread unwinds over the top of the spool while the spool stays stationary, usually fixed with a cap to keep it from sliding off the pin.

The straight-wound spool is intended to rotate on the vertical pin as the thread unwinds straight from the side of the spool and flows directly into the thread path without any waves or curls.

If used improperly, the thread unwinds in an unnatural way, causing curls and kinks that can tighten and coil as they get closer to the needle. The thread breaks as the kink tries to feed through the eye of the needle. This is especially true with delicate threads, such as metallic and soft polyesters.

A thread stand should be used only for cross-wound spools. The vertical post does not allow a stacked spool to rotate so the thread feeds over the top, creating coils.

# Start Your Engines

Heirloom machine quilting does not require a fancy computerized sewing machine or extensive attachments. A well-conditioned sewing machine is equally as important as the skill the quilter acquires when practicing with the suggested supplies. Learn how to care for your machine; clean and oil the bobbin area if recommended. Investigate the accessories that came with your machine and what they can do.

Sounds simple enough. So many students admit that they didn't know they had a certain foot or attachment, or they bought one six years ago and never used it. If you have it, use it!

Remember, if your machine has more than one spool pin, learn why and use them. The type of thread, as well as the way it is wound on the spool (cross-wound or straight-wound) will determine which spool pin is used.

# Driving Without Traction

Remember that the stitch-length setting on the machine does not apply when the feed dogs are lowered and therefore not advancing the fabric. The length of a stitch is entirely dependent on how fast you move the fabric with your hands compared to the speed the machine is stitching, which is controlled by the pressure of your foot on the foot pedal.

With machines that do not have the option of lowering the feed dogs, set the stitch length at zero, so at least the feed dogs will not be attempting to move the fabric. Cover the feed dogs with a piece of plastic the thickness of a credit card. One student with a Featherweight couldn't lower the feed dogs, so she used the Supreme Slider, which not only covered the feed dogs, but also made the machine bed slippery.

My Featherweight with Supreme Slider.

# Shock Absorbers

For free-motion quilting, use a darning foot or open-toed free-motion foot. Keep in mind that this is refined work, and a small foot will provide a better view. Here are a variety of styles of darning feet and why you use each one:

A regular darning foot may have come with your machine. It is fine to try out free-motion quilting with it, but you may want to invest in another foot type. The big plastic foot can be used for anchoring the layers, echo quilting, and raw-edge quilting, like landscape quilting. This large darning foot is a good choice for anchoring the top. Its broad surface flattens a wide path for stitching. Some quilters use the circular ridges in the plastic as a guide for echo quilting. Landscape quilters who encounter fraying of the raw edges use this foot to tame them.

The metal free-motion foot was designed for heirloom machine quilters. It is tiny and provides just a slight touch to hold the layers during the formation of the stitch, yet it allows for the best view of the needle and stitching area.

Recently, a student called me to say she was attending my upcoming free-motion class in which she intended to use her 25-year-old Necchi, only to discover it didn't have a darning foot. I suggested that she try to either remodel a foot from her machine or find a darning foot from a different brand. By the time I arrived at the class, she had experimented with darning feet from several different manufacturers and had found one that worked. Her machine not only functioned with that foot, the stitches it formed were among the nicest in the room.

# Walking Foot

At times, I use a walking foot to stitch the straight lines in a project, to increase the accuracy of a grid, or to stitch a foundation around patchwork blocks before I use free-motion quilting for the curvilinear motifs and meandering.

The stitches made with the walking foot may look different from the free-motion work, which may be objectionable or of little consequence to your piece. When using the walking foot, set the stitch length to match your free-motion stitches.

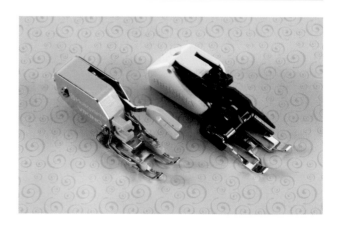

# Single-Hole Stitch Plate

Single-hole stitch plates are sold as accessories for zigzag machines that have wide openings to allow the needle to move from side to side. The single-hole plate keeps the quilting surface as flat as possible when stitching and prevents the fabric from being pushed down into the larger opening. They are also great for refined free-motion quilting and when stitching triangular patchwork pieces together.

The plate on the left is the single-hole plate, and the one on the right is for zigzag stitching.

## A Better View

Try placing two doorstops purchased at the hardware store under the back edge of your sewing machine. They will tilt the machine to give you a better view of the needle.

# Thread

What a big new world of thread there is out there, and the choice of which thread to use may be much more important than you realize. Trust me on this. There are reasons manufacturers invest in each type they produce. Select threads according to the effect you are attempting to achieve, based on the end use of the project. The heavier the thread, the more durable it will be and the more attention it will attract to itself.

The weight of the thread also affects the size of the stitch you can make. Consider choosing thread as if you were choosing a vehicle to drive. Using heavy thread would be like trying to maneuver a dump truck on a track designed for a tricycle. The size of your thread and the stitch length impact your ability to master tiny curved lines for stippling and intricate designs. To get nice curves, you need a lot of tiny stitches. Regardless of your thread choice, do a test piece, auditioning the thread on the fabric to see if you approve the final effect and to perfect your tension.

Matching the color of the thread to the fabric is a matter of preference. If the exact color to match the fabric cannot be found, I prefer a shade darker. Here is an example of thread that was too light, and to me, the leaf outline looks like an X-ray.

The process of machine quilting requires a lot of thread, so be sure to have a sufficient supply on hand. High-quality thread is worth every penny, and it eliminates the problems that the cheap brands can create. Many designs used for heirloom machine quilting require that the same line be stitched more than once. When fine or invisible thread is used, a line of stitching can be retraced without an unsightly thread build-up.

Thread labels can be confusing. Thread sizing is not standardized. The higher the number, the finer the thread is; for example, 100 is very lightweight. Many manufacturers are now offering 60-weight threads in either two or three plies, indicated on the label as 60/2 or 60/3. A two-ply thread is lighter in weight than a three-ply.

Here are my choices for the finest, lightest-weight threads:

The Bottom Line by Superior Threads is a two-ply, 60 weight, lint-free polyester thread. I use it in the top of the machine, as well as the bobbin. It is available in a wide variety of colors, on large spools, and is reasonably priced.

YLI manufactures wonderful silk thread in 100 weight, which can be used in the top and bobbin. It has a sheen that is perfect with elegant fabric. YLI also makes Heirloom Cotton Thread in 70 weight (the 100 is too light for me). It is less expensive than the silk and can be used for both the top and the bobbin. It has a more traditional look when used on dull cotton fabric. When silk is used for top thread, Bottom Line is a good choice for the bobbin to save your cash for more books.

Invisible thread is used in the top of the machine with a lightweight thread in the bobbin. Many machine quilters use invisible thread to achieve a hand-quilted effect. It is available in "clear" for quilting light-colored fabrics and "smoke" for more colorful fabrics. It may be made in polyester or nylon. Invisible thread can get old and turn brittle. If it is breaking, buy new.

## Computerized machines

When using very lightweight thread in one of my new computerized machines, my stitching was frequently interrupted because the machine was mistakenly indicating a broken top thread. I had to go into the setup menu and turn off the thread sensor feature.

## Bobbin Thread

If you haven't yet used lightweight thread in the bobbin, you will be amazed at the difference it will make in your work. Choose a color to match either the top thread or the backing fabric and use several different colors for the same quilt if you feel that looks best. Lightweight thread goes a long way when filling a bobbin. If you purchased only one small spool, fill it only half full to save some for the top of the machine.

Use bobbins that are made specifically for your machine by the manufacturer. Be sure that they fill evenly. It is imperative for proper tension and nicely formed stitches.

# Machine Tension

Of all of the little details we are covering, proper machine tension is the most critical for perfectly formed stitches. Lightweight threads require the machine to stitch with thread different from what it was calibrated to use. The factory usually sets the tension for 40-weight, 3-ply thread. Learn to adjust the upper tension to accommodate thinner threads, if necessary. Consult the owner's manual and make minor adjustments.

Always test the threads and needles to get the tension correct before stitching on the quilt. Every time you change threads or the bobbin, do a new test. Make a quilt sandwich from the exact fabrics and batting used for each project as a practice sample.

The top thread should form little rounded humps that catch the bobbin thread in the middle of the quilt layers. We don't want to see little dots of bobbin thread on the top, nor do we want one thread pulling the other flat along the fabric.

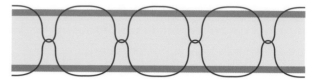

When the tension is correct, both threads lock in the middle of the layers.

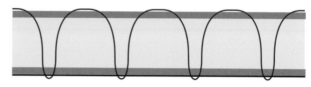

The top tension is too loose or the bobbin tension is too tight.

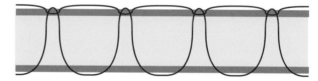

The top tension is too tight or the bobbin is too loose.

The illustrations above show common tension problems and the adjustments to remedy them. Make adjustments in tiny increments and remember to make a note of where the tension was set for regular sewing, as well as the settings for perfect tension with each different thread, and reset it for regular setting when you are finished. Remember: righty tighty, lefty loosie.

If your machine has a removable bobbin case, with a setscrew on the side, it may need to be adjusted for differing thread weights. To test the tension, place the bobbin in the case with the thread through the tension spring and the case in the palm of your hand. Now, pull on the thread. If the case can be lifted out of your hand by the thread, the tension is too tight. If the case stays in you hand and the bobbin spins, it is too loose. With proper tension, the bobbin should be lifted out of your palm and then ease down with a slight jerk on the thread. If you are uncomfortable with adjusting the tension screw on your bobbin case, purchase an additional one and adjust it for lightweight threads.

# Needles

Choose the needle size and type according to the size and style of thread. With fine thread, use a small needle to produce small stitches. For 50- or 60-weight thread, use a 70 or 80 needle. For 100-weight thread, use a 60, 70, or 75 needle.

Some machine-quilting teachers are using embroidery needles, and others recommend topstitch or universal needles. I have had success with sharps or Microtex. Experiment with several and use whichever one works best for your situation.

Begin any quilting project with a new needle and change it after eight hours of stitching. If you are experiencing snagged threads or skipped stitches, try another new needle. It could be a bad needle right out of the pack.

Now, one last thing before you begin to stitch on your good piece—the warm-up. Each time you quilt, spend a few minutes stitching on a practice sandwich first. Adjust the tension and spend as much time as needed to get your body moving to produce a consistent look across the quilt surface. Stitch some doodles and some stippling, trying to match the scale and spacing you used the last time you stitched.

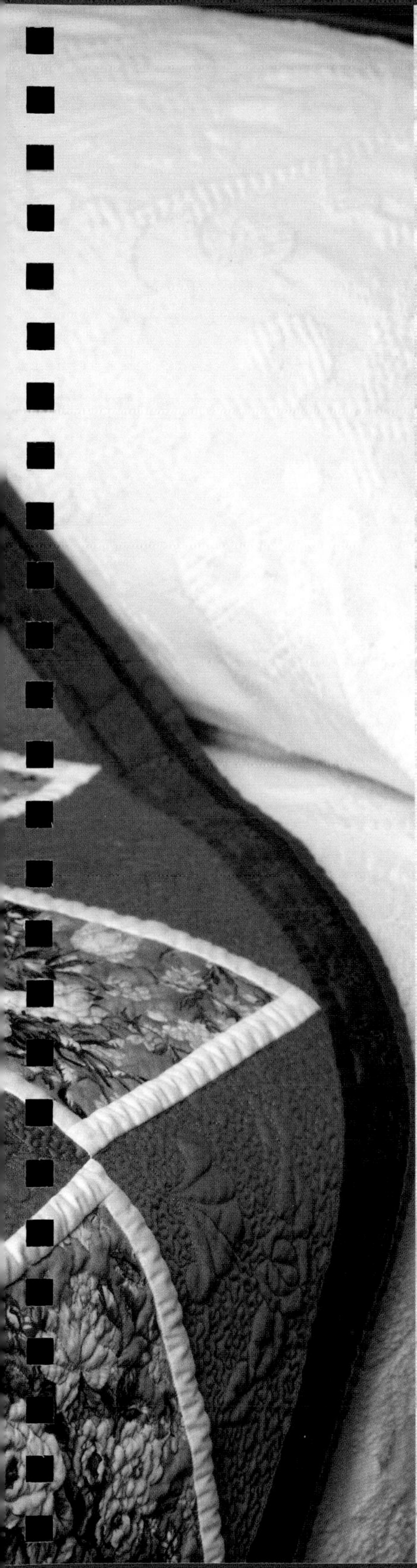

*Step Five:*

# High-Performance Stitching

What are we really doing when we use lines of stitching to hold our quilt layers together? We are, in reality, adding information to the quilt surface, just as you would if you were writing or drawing lines on a piece of paper. I say, let's give artistic purpose to the function of holding the layers together.

# Step It Up

At a recent quilt show, I couldn't help noticing that several nicely pieced quilts disappointed me because the quilters had missed the mark when it came to the quilting details. The quilts lacked the punch they could easily have had if the maker had just followed these simple guidelines for distinctive quilting:

If your intent is to enhance the patchwork you worked so hard to create, use the seam lines as quilting paths to increase their presence and give full impact to your work. Then create powerful contrast by adding background fillers, which will make the light bounce off the crisp edges of the raised patchwork as the background recedes into the shadows. Find the courage to bump the filler right up against the patchwork. If you don't, the effect of the robust graphic patchwork will be lost. The information that remains (a baggie outline and less distinct points) will confuse the eye.

You have all the information needed, and it's time to imprint the quilting design on your brain, put on the darning foot, lower the feed dogs and presser foot, and make a test of the thread tension to get it perfect. Whew! You are finally ready to start free-motion stitching.

## Look Down the Road

What I am about to tell you may seem so simple you may wonder why it's taking up space here. But, the needle will always stitch in exactly the same place, so you don't need to look where it is stitching. Instead, you need to look ahead at the marked stitching line to know where you are driving next.

*OPPOSITE PAGE: Ivy Wreath Pattern, 2005*

## Where to Start

Knowing how and where to start a line of stitching is an important element in the overall success of your project. Whenever possible, begin in an area of the design that will be covered by later stitching.

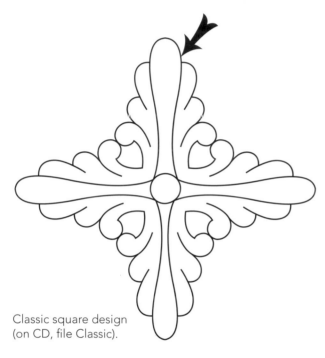

Classic square design (on CD, file Classic).

*1* Insert the needle into the quilt where you want to start stitching. Then rotate the flywheel one entire turn, stopping with the needle at its highest point. This will bring up a loop of bobbin thread so you can pull it through to the top of the quilt.

*2* Return the needle into the fabric. Hold both threads out of the way and make about five or six stitches very close together to secure the thread. (Using too many stitches in the exact same place will cause an unsightly build-up of thread.)

*3* Begin stitching with a normal stitch length, following the marked line for about 3" from where you began.

*4* Stop with the needle down. Clip the beginning thread tails at the surface of the quilt.

*5* Begin stitching again. Coordinate the speed of the machine with the movement of your hands.

*6* Focus on the direction you are moving, not on the needle.

*7* Vary the machine's speed with the intricacy of the design. Any time you are unsure of where to proceed, take your foot off the pedal and stop with the needle down.

## Ending the Stitches

To finish a line of stitching, simply take about five or six stitches very close together, raise the pressure foot, and snip off the threads.

If you unexpectedly run out of bobbin thread, clip the top thread and begin the new line of stitching ½" back, right on top of the previously stitched line.

# My Faves from Mr. Scissors

Well-known to quilt-show goers, vendor Mr. Scissors carries these snips, which were originally made for the medical industry for eye surgery, but they have been modified for quilters. The fine tips allow you to get underneath tiny stitches, and the curved blade ensures that you won't cut the fabric when you snip off thread ends. The spring action makes them easy to use whether you are left- or right- handed.

Both styles of the large-ring, micro-tip scissors have blades so fine they can even slip under the tiniest stitches. These comfortable scissors are perfect for detailed appliqué, embroidery, and quilting projects.

# Handling the Quilt Bundle

People ask me how I get a big quilt into that little space under the arm of the machine. Until they have experienced the freedom that free-motion quilting allows, they assume that the process is much harder than it really is. They may think that, because they need to rotate their work when the feed dogs are engaged for garment sewing or patchwork, then they struggle to flip that big quilt sandwich at every turn.

To begin with, I do not roll the quilt sandwich, nor do I use any sort of clip to keep it under control. I am most concerned that the weight of the quilt be supported on the tabletop so there is no stress on the area under the needle. To secure the quilt into sections, I need access to the entire quilt surface, so I make sure that the table (or several tables if one is not big enough) supports the whole quilt. I then clear and smooth the area for stitching as I come to it. For this process, I may readjust, and possibly rotate, the quilt to be able to move it freely along the stitching lines. Then for the free-motion quilting, I create a "puddle" of space, about a foot square, to work in for the first motif. After stitching the first motif, I move to the next one and make a puddle of space for it, and so on.

With free-motion quilting, it is no longer necessary to rotate the quilt. You can stitch in any direction within a section. When working in the center of a large piece, you may want to loosely fold the right side of the bundle into accordion pleats to have better access to the needle. Depending on the quilt's size, you may also have some of the quilt resting in your lap. When you get to the motifs and details of the outer borders, you will want to turn the piece so that most of the quilt is resting on your left, giving you easy access to the working area.

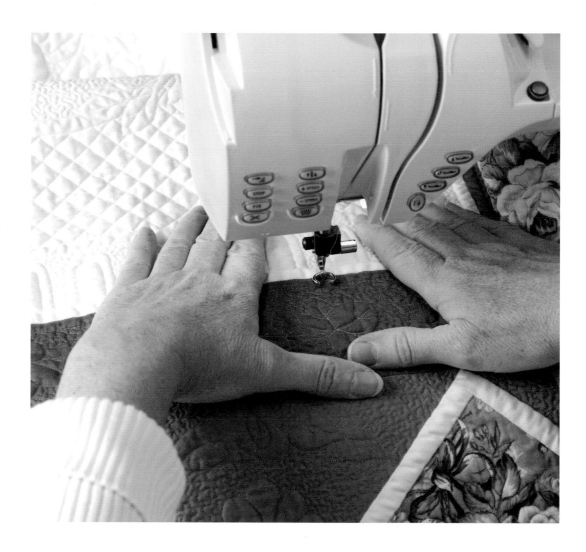

## Get a Grip!

I want you to become conscious of how you are positioning your hands on the quilt. Make sure you can see the area you need to drive to without extending your neck. Also, be sure that the design area is well lit. Find a position that allows your elbows, wrists, and shoulders to relax. Make adjustments to the height of your chair and to the lighting. Hopefully, you will be having so much fun you will lose track of time. You don't want your body to be all locked up without realizing it.

When I am free-motion quilting, there are times when my hands are resting flat against the fabric so I can slide the quilt across the bed of the machine. At other times, I grab a fold of fabric to move the bundle. Use the grip (or gloves) that you feel provides the best control in each situation. Remember, when you need to pause or stop, keep your hands on the fabric until the needle is down (to securely hold the fabric layers) and take your foot off the gas.

# Traveling from Place to Place

Getting from place to place on the quilt top should be considered before you are in the middle of stitching and find yourself unsure of how to get to the next design. There are times when you can travel from one motif to the next with a line of stippling or another background filler.

Or, if the area you are working on is close to the outside edge of the quilt, you may drive along the edge where the stitching will be hidden in the binding.

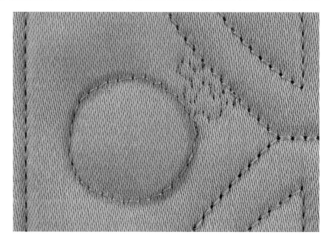

## Jump Stitches

Using a jump stitch is another helpful way to travel if the new area to be stitched is not too far away. After completing the stitching in one area, secure your stitches and raise the needle and presser foot. The thread should be loose enough to allow you to slide the fabric a few inches to the new area you want to stitch. Insert the needle, secure the thread, and continue to stitch, being cautious not to stitch over the jumped thread. After the stitching in that area is finished, trim the thread ends even with the surface of the quilt.

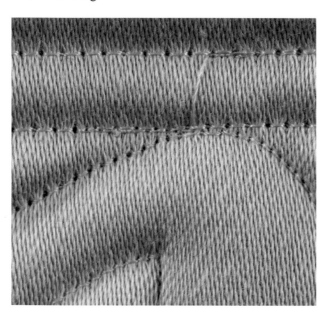

# Retracing

There are times when it is necessary to retrace a section of a previously quilted line. When the design calls for this, stitch the line to the place where retracing is necessary, stop with the needle down and look at the previously stitched line, not the needle. Carefully back out, using the same tire tracks, and guide the needle over the top of the first stitches.

## Practice Makes Perfect

Practice retracing the rope design from the CD. Slowly follow the pattern without thread in the machine. When you can steer the needle right on top of the first line of stitching, try altering the speed of the machine to see how that affects your accuracy for staying on the line. The faster the machine runs, the smaller the stitches are if you don't change the speed your hands are moving.

# Removing Unwanted Stitches

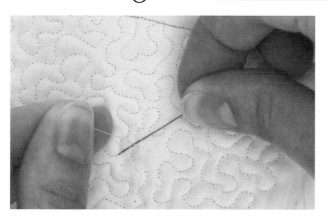

When removing unwanted stitches, work from the back of the quilt to prevent any possibility of damaging the quilt surface. Find a place where a seam ripper can be slipped under a stitch. Cut the stitch then loosen the next stitch, using a straight pin if necessary. Coax enough stitches loose and eventually you will be able to grab the end of the bobbin thread. Pull on that thread to pull the top thread to the back. Continue tugging and removing stitches until the mistake is gone.

## Seam ripper gripper

Wrap a wide rubber band around your seam ripper or stiletto to help grip the narrow handle.

## Running off the road

Here is my remedy for steering too far off a marked line. Stop stitching as soon as you notice you are off the line. Don't secure your thread. Secure a new thread ½" before the mistake occurred and continue quilting on the line to complete the design. Pull out the off-road stitches, back to where you retraced them.

# Step Away from the Vehicle

Know when to take a break. Mistakes and poor stitching quality happen when your muscles tense up or your eyes get tired. Take a break and visit your loved ones, they probably miss you!

You are learning so much, and I am so excited to provide you these hints to make free-motion more fun. I want you to experience the joy of creating quilted treasures completely with your own hands. Free-motion quilting takes practice, but anything that you have a passion for can be achieved. Put your heart into it!

## Step Six:

# Stitching Backgrounds

When we take a closer look at the surface of a well-planned quilt, the quilting designs and background fillers can take us on an adventure of discovery. Filling backgrounds with interesting patterns is not only possible with machine quilting, I encourage it.

The background fillers can take command with a distinct purpose or create a silent foundation that allows dominant images to shine. They can play a role in expressing the style of a quilt. In this step, you will learn to determine which fillers are based on a marked framework and which are directed by a pattern imprinted on your brain. We will also cover the versatility of stippling and grids.

This sample from a fabric painting class shows simple stitching patterns that add variety to the piece. I cut several simple stencils to indicate the outlines of leaves and then lightly added metallic paint to the base fabric with a stencil brush. When the paint was dry and heat-set, I stitched the filler patterns to add information that reads like multiple leaf textures.

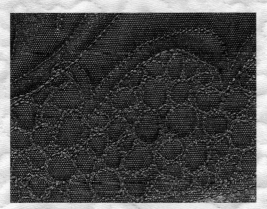
Circular stitching creates tiny pebbles.

Curved lines of stitching fill the leaf.

Curling stitches create another filler.

Fillers include numerous patterns, which I divide into two groups: free form, in which the stitching is simply directed by a pattern imprinted on the brain; and formal, with marked lines or grids.

### Frolicking Fills

Long-arm and home-machine quilters are inventing many creative patterns that they use to fill empty spaces around motifs or all over an entire quilt top. There are many books and patterns available now to inspire you.

Free-form background fillers require little or no marking on the quilt top. Rather, these patterns are stitched from ideas in your mind. They are random, not perfect, repeated forms. The patterns are as numerous and varied as the people who stitch them.

## Free-form Landscape Patterns

Free-form quilting is ideal for landscape quilts. Here is an example with several fillers, lightly dancing around the surface of a fabric I tie-dyed in a class. The quilted lines of colored thread offer the viewer information to read.

Look closely at the outlines of some of the leaves and grass. The paint isn't quite filled in, but by stitching the outline in the color of the foliage, the eye fills in with information that isn't really there.

### Atmospheric Conditions, Clouds and Wind

Quilting lines can be used to create a sense of movement that, in reality, can't be seen. These lines of stitching look like what we imagine if we could see the wind blow.

*OPPOSITE PAGE: Landscape quilts are ideal for free-form quilting. It is possible to create image where it does not exist, or enhance existing fabric design.*

*Details of free-motion quilting.*

# Intentional Communication

Adding artistic expression to the function of holding the layers of your quilt together takes thought. What will these lines of threads do to enhance the quilt surface? The stitching can convey information by using images and letters, or it can simply create background space. The eye translates the stitched lines into a message for the brain to recognize. We are giving the audience information to read.

**Lines Can Create Movement**

If the lines of stitching you use to fill the background do something other than follow the seam lines in a patchwork quilt top, make your objective intentional. The examples in the photos show how quilting lines are allowed to have their own voice. Anchoring the layers together is their mission, but creating movement is their purpose.

My thanks to RaNae Merrill (quilt designer and quiltmaker) and Linda Taylor (machine quilting) who made SAILS AND WAVES (84" x 108") which demonstrates how the patchwork was disregarded when the quilting plan was devised. Linda quilted curving lines that fill the combined area of several geometric shapes.

In this example, look at the placement of several different motifs in this circular setting. The simple straight lines used to fill the empty corner space create a radiant burst. They provide an orderly movement that allows the motifs to be the focal point of the quilt.

Radiant Elements Quilt, 2007.

# Creating a Quiet Zone

Quilts that are heirloom machine quilted usually include background quilting, which fills the negative space around the designs with dense stitching. Fillers create contrast with puffy motifs by flattening the background space.

For my contest quilts, which have complicated layouts, I most often rely on stippling or grids as background fillers. Both recede into the background, while functioning to anchor the layers. Their formality allows the graphic images of my elegant layouts to take center stage. The density of the stippled background must contrast with the motif.

# Meandering, Stippling and Micro Stippling

A person out wandering a winding trail is said to be meandering. In machine quilting, meandering has a different identity. It is a large-scale continuous line of stitching that fills the fabric with puzzle-piece and wormlike shapes. The difference between stippling and meandering is the scale of the work. When the lines are less than ¼" apart, they are referred to as stip-

pling. Micro stippling is very tiny stippling.

Stippling establishes a quiet zone that allows the designs to have a strong voice and gives the eye a place to rest within the activity of all the other images.

One great way to understand what stippling is supposed to look like is to study photographs of stippling to see the different styles.

Meandering adds texture to these sewing room accessories.

Two different sizes of stippling are used to add contrast to the background.

I hear a lot of comments from viewers about my tiny, precise stippling. I tell them it takes a tiny needle and lightweight thread, and I don't move very far between each stitch. If you have ever stitched tiny doll clothes or, better yet, the tiny fingers of a doll's hand, you know that you need to have a very short stitch length.

Look at the lengths of the dashes in the illustration. They show that small stitches make nice curving lines, whereas long stitches make choppy-looking stippling. Longer stitches are just fine for meandering, but they don't allow the creation of smooth curves for smaller stippling

There's another reason the stitches may look choppy. The quilt sandwich may not be gliding over the machine surface. The backing fabric may be sticky, or there may be too much drag from the weight of the piece. Pull more of the quilt up to rest on the table and create a "puddle" of quilt unencumbered by the weight of the piece. Backing fabric can be spray starched, and you can use a slider to increase the slipperiness of the machine bed.

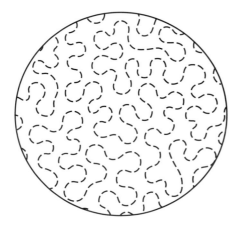
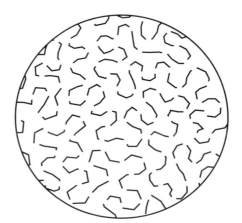

# If You Can Draw It, You Can Stitch It

Tracing a design, whether it is from a stencil or a paper design, imprints on your brain the shapes you will stitch. Repeatedly tracing the design with your finger or a marking tool is beneficial because you will learn a driving plan while you trace.

Stippling is used to fill in open space and is not drawn on the quilt. But, you are just learning and need to understand how the lines turn and bend before you can steer the sewing machine down that road. Here is a good way to practice stippling:

*1* Print out the Stippling Exercise from the CD.

*2* Spend some time tracing it with your finger. Study how the bumps and wormlike lines create an unpredictable path.

*3* Trace it again without lifting your finger from the paper, and you will make the connection that stippling is one continuous line that may be a very long and winding road.

*4* Next, use a water-soluble marker to trace the stippling guide on a piece of practice fabric, pin basted with batting and backing.

*5* Adjust the tension of your machine for lightweight thread then follow the traced lines with free-motion quilting.

*6* Now try stippling on a piece of fabric that's not marked.

*7* Then try stippling around some motifs drawn on a practice quilt sandwich. Make sure the stippling touches the outlines of the motifs.

Practice until you become comfortable with the technique. Soon you can begin to develop your own style. Your stippling will look good no matter what shapes you use as long as the shapes you are stitching and the distance between the lines are consistent. As you continue to practice, you can refine the size of your stitching, from meandering, to stippling, to micro stippling.

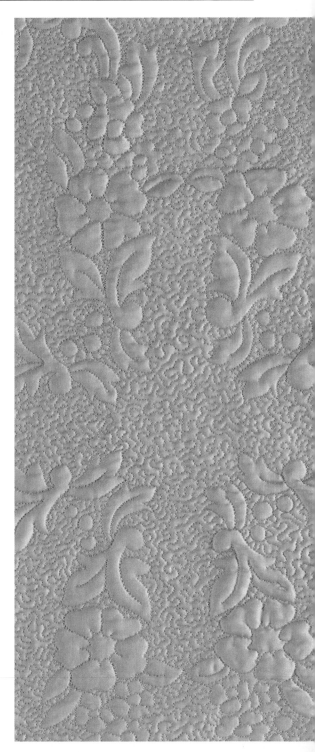

Remember these hints when you are working on a project:

- Stippling is not drawn on the quilt, just filled in after the motifs have been stitched.

- Visualize the blank space to be filled with stippling before you begin stitching.

- Start stitching at the bottom of the area you want to fill and work away from yourself. This will give you the best view of where you have been and where you need to go next.

- Background stippling should touch the edges of the motifs and fill the space up to the binding of the quilt.

- The closer the rows are, the more time it will take to stitch them and the more thread you will use.

- All quilting should be evenly distributed throughout your entire quilt. Uneven amounts of quilting will distort the quilt and cause wavy edges. Areas that are left without quilting will look unfinished.

## Maneuvering in Narrow Spaces

Here is my simple trick for avoiding an unsightly zigzagging river when filling a narrow space with stippling between two motifs. The stitching is approaching the area from the top left, fill the entire space between from one side all the way to the other side. When you reach the bottom, just retrace the outline of the motif on the fight back up to the top.

## Micro-Stippling Exercise

Imagine you have a sheet of typing paper and you need to write a note in cursive that contains sixteen words. Simple, right? Now imagine you need to write the same message on a tiny sticky note. You would need to refine your focus and write in tiny letters. That is just what is necessary for micro stippling: refined focus.

Practice tiny stippling when you are talking on the phone or just sitting at your desk. Print out the StipplingExercise from the CD. Study the printed guide and follow it with your finger. Now fill a sheet of paper with stippling; don't lift your pencil. When you are ready, try filling a tiny sticky note with micro stippling. Try it first on scrap paper, and then try it on your practice quilt.

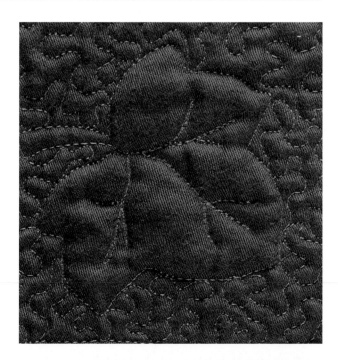

# Formal Fillers

Formal fillers may require some amount of marking. They fill background space following marked curved or straight lines, or a grid line.

Some fillers are created by just stitching straight lines, but many have a marked grid.

These lines may be followed with stitching to create checkerboards, basket weaves, and square- or diamond-shaped crossed lines. The intersections of a marked grid may also be used as guides for creating repeated curved designs.

## Parallel Lanes of Traffic

Channel quilting features a series of evenly spaced, straight parallel lines of stitching. They can stand alone to fill an entire area or be used as support to back up other designs. They are also used to provide a geometric contrast to curved motifs.

## Echo Quilting

With echo quilting, the outer shape of a motif is followed by rows of stitched lines that are equally distant from each other. When numerous rows are used, they give the effect of tiny ripples on the surface of a lake. Use just a row or two, or stitch as many rows as it takes to fill the background space between the shapes.

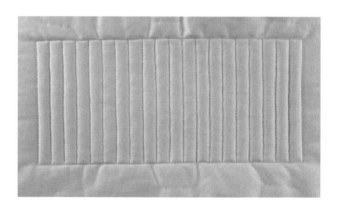

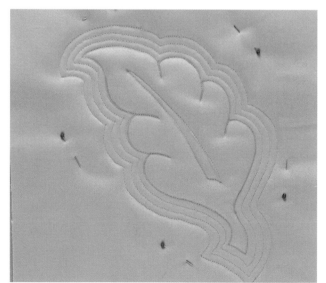

A grid is used to fill the background of this CD carrying case.

# Stitching Grids

Straight-line grids can be stitched over an entire patchwork top or used to fill specifically planned areas of a project. Often used with appliqué, they create a strong contrast to curved shapes.

Grid lines can be drawn parallel to the edges of the quilt or on the diagonal, with varying degrees of angle. Grids can be free-motion quilted or stitched with the aid of a walking foot. Free-motion stitches may look different from those formed with a walking foot, so if you are using both types, you must decide if that is of consequence to your project.

There are two important factors for successful grids, keeping the lines straight and keeping ripples from forming in the fabric. Stitching neighboring rows in opposite directions causes ripples and puckers. This is of particular concern with fabric that has sheen, like sateen or silk.

Here are some tips for successful grid quilting:

- Study the best path with your finger before you begin stitching.
- Number your travel plan on a paper pattern.
- Stitch each line from one end all the way to the motif outline or the fabric edge. No detours!
- For projects that are small enough to rotate easily, turn the piece in the same direction for the entire stitching process. Keep track of the direction by marking directional arrows with a washout marker.
- Grids often require some retracing of a motif outline to get to the next grid line. You can use jump stitches to travel also.
- For two rows that are next to each other, stitch one then go back to the beginning of the line so you can stitch the second row in the same direction.

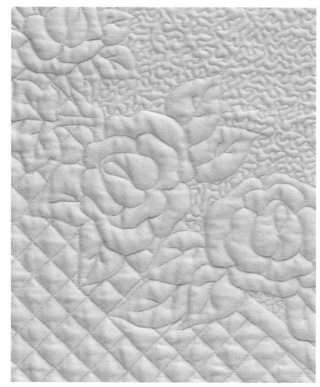

Geometric grids contrast the curving shapes of the thread illustration.

## Stitch Length

Remember, if you are using a walking foot for anchoring the straight lines of a project that will also have free-motion curvy designs, set the machine stitch length similar to the length of your free-motion stitches.

## Straight Lines

Use a little ruler to help you stitch straight lines.

# Stitching Contained Grids

We need to consider the space to be filled to determine where to begin stitching. If the grid is contained in an outlined space, like a circle, square, rectangle, or oval, stitch the outline first during the anchoring process. If the space to be filled is defined by a border design, that design is stitched before the grid.

Here are the steps for stitching a grid within a square or rectangular shape:

**1** Starting on the outline of the shape, secure your thread ¼" away from the top-right corner.

**2** Stitch the entire outline of the square or rectangle, ending the thread ¼" past the place where you started. Stop with the needle down.

**3** Continuing with the same thread, stitch along the outline to the intersection of the closest grid line. Follow that line to its end. Stop with the needle down.

**4** Pivot 90 degrees (rotating the fabric if using a walking foot) and stitch the line. End with the needle down.

**5** Pivot again and travel along the outline or jump to the next grid line and stitch it to the end. Stop with the needle down.

**6** Continue in this manner until the entire grid is filled. (You can divide large sections in half, if needed.)

# Square Grid Example

This illustration shows a numbered diagram for stitching a grid that is contained in a square outline. Dotted lines outside the outline indicate where to begin and end thread.

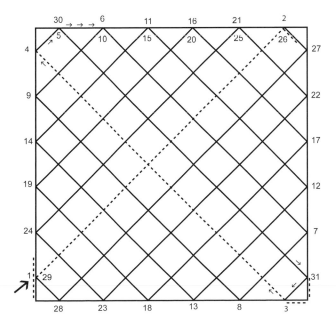

If there is a motif or design in the center of the space to be grid quilted, stitch the motif and its outline, if it has one, before stitching the grid. When the motif has been completed, follow the same procedure described for a grid inside a contained space (page 87). When the line of stitching hits the outline of the central design, retrace short distances on the outline or use a jump stitch to hop over the design. Secure the thread and continue to stitch the same grid line as though the design was not there.

This same concept of stitching the motifs first and then filling in the grid works when a grid is contained within a border of motifs.

# Mark a Grid to Wander

Study this wonderful background pattern that's based on the pumpkin seed design seen in Amish quilts. My teacher Diane Gaudynski perfected a method of doing it on the machine by drawing a grid on the quilt then stitching arcs from one grid intersection to the next. Diane playfully calls the pattern Dianeshenko. Many other designs can be developed with this concept.

Now, that is plenty to get you started filling in background spaces and stitching grids. Remember the following points: Keep the distribution of stitched areas as equal as possible across the entire surface of the quilt. Uneven amounts will distort the quilt and cause wavy edges. Areas that are left without quilting will look unfinished. Any background-quilting pattern that you decide to use should touch the edges of the motifs and fill the space up to the quilt binding.

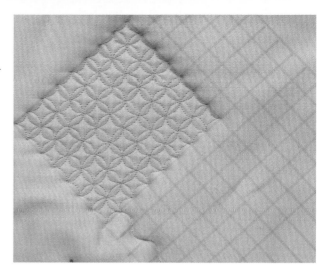

## Step Seven:

# Crossing the Finish Line

Step seven, the final lap of our journey—in the previous steps, I have offered the strategies and solutions you need for successful free-motion quilting. Once you have learned the basics, I encourage you to elevate your standards in every phase of the quiltmaking process. Expect more of yourself, from the planning of the layout, to the completion of the binding. Set some higher goals. Choose more complicated designs, and move beyond your current skill level. What would any teacher tell her students when they were about to embark on a new experience? If you really want something, make it a priority and put your heart into it.

*OPPOSITE PAGE: Huron Quilts, 2007, printable designs on CD.*

# Free-Motion Reality Check

Are you among the masses that are afraid of losing control if you lower the feed dogs? Do you believe you will ruin your quilt top if you try free-motion quilting on it? Let's get some perspective here. If you have the courage to drive a car out in traffic every day, what scares you so about quilting? It's only fabric!

You may assume, as I once did, that after a little instruction, you should be able to quilt beautifully. I went home after one six-hour free-motion class and didn't practice for months. Then, when I finally tried to quilt again, I was very disappointed. What made me think I could do this without practicing?

Stitching with the feed dogs engaged and with a regular foot on the machine is like first-grade printing, and stitching free motion with the feed dogs lowered is like cursive writing. I ask you, didn't they have us practicing our cursive writing every day for all of third grade? So what made me think I could go to one free-motion class and be successful? Learning to quilt takes time, knowledge, practice, and commitment. Having the freedom to run that machine with accuracy and control is exhilarating! The effort is so rewarding and worth every minute of practice.

Revel in the fact that you bring more to this challenge than you may realize. Everything you have done in your quilting life up until this day adds to your machine quilting foundation. For several years after that first class, I lived a life without curves and was chained to my walking foot. I relied on it while chastising myself for not being brave enough to try the curved-line designs I wanted so badly to stitch. What I didn't realize was, by just stitching in the ditch, I was gaining valuable knowledge of how to maneuver the quilt sandwich under the needle.

You, too, can free-motion quilt. I wrote the seven steps so that, if you go to a class or study on your own, you won't have to try to remember everything. It's all here for your reference any time you are ready to make the commitment to learn. Now, with these steps to follow and my encouragement, you will be on your way to completing your own quilts.

## Keep Trying

A dance teacher on TV advised her students to take a class at least three times before deciding if dancing was right for them.

# Abandoning the Express Train

Think how much more enjoyable quilting could be if you slowed down. Discover the adventure of the road trip at a relaxing pace, in a comfortable vehicle, rather than speeding past the many fun experiences you could have.

Approach machine quilting with an open mind. I encounter people in this fast-paced world who are mass-producing tops without any intension of making them into quilts. They are locked into the mind-set that they can't do free-motion quilting. They won't even try, so they let some-one else make quilts out of their tops. And some people make quilts at a crazed pace, trying to get them over with as fast as possible.

Slow down; find the enjoyment in what you're doing. Consider focusing on quality rather than quantity. Try to relax from the tension of the demands others impose on your time. What's the worst thing that could happen if you tell everyone that you want to quilt this weekend, then just locked the sewing room door?

# Dispelling Machine-Quilting Myths

## Throttle Wide Open

If anyone ever told you that free-motion quilting could only happen at full speed, forget that notion. It is incorrect. You have my permission to use whatever speed you are comfortable with, and you will certainly want to slow down for intricate patterns. Adjust the speed of the machine to the movement of the quilt with your hands, depending on the difficulty of the path you are following.

## Jumping the Track

You may have been led to believe the falsehood that stitching one isolated object (even a simple shape like a heart in the middle of a plain square) is easier than an intricate design adorned with embellishments and background fillers.

Think about it. If you go off the line of a perfect lonely heart, you are pretty much out of luck because it will be easily seen. You either have to look at the mistake for eternity or rip it out. Here is a little secret for you: the more there is to look at, the more there is to distract the eye from any problems.

The following illustration shows another example of "more is better." You might assume that the irregular outline of the leaf is difficult to stitch. But, like the heart example, you can fool the eye with more to look at. See how, because of the little jaggy outline, no one could tell if you made a mistake.

Consider this, if the leaves to be stitched are irregular sizes or have jagged edges, who will know exactly where the edge was supposed to be once the marked line is washed away? And, depending on the shape of the object, and if you are using a background filler, you might be able to repair the boo-boo with stippling.

## My Way or the Highway!

Some of my students say that a previous teacher told them to do something a certain way. I suggest that you do whatever works best for your situation. That teacher's process may have worked well for her, but better ways of doing things are being presented every day. If you find a better idea for something I've shown you, by all means, do it and tell me about your successes. I have a tips page on my website (www.heirloomquiltingdesigns.com) for information that people send me.

## There's More Than One Route

At Harriet Hargrave's Machine Quilting Celebration, students have the opportunity to take quilting classes from several teachers. Just by chance, on the last day of the event, I was teaching how I stitch a "string of beads," which is a row of circles between two lines. One student spoke up to say that the three teachers she had during the week all quilted the design differently.

Diane Gaudynski approaches the beads pattern by stitching a row of half circles on the first pass then completing the other half of the circles on the return pass.

Lee Cleland stitches a complete circle, beginning at the point the bead touches the line on which it rests. She then travels along the line to the next circle.

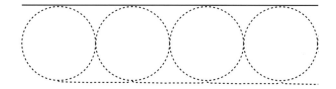

At that time, I was using figure eights, stitching the top half of one bead then the bottom half of the next, all the way across the row. I then stitched the other half of each circle on the return trip. After I heard how Lee stitched them, I switched to her method. I felt I could form better circles that way, and I didn't mind retracing along the outline. We can all learn from one another.

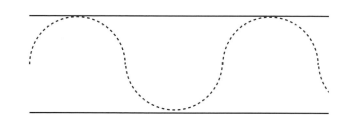

# Recommended Reading

We can also benefit from the wisdom of many teachers. Their differing techniques and experiences are available to us in many books. I believe that those who quilt on a home sewing machine can benefit from reading information from a long-arm quilter and vice versa. Investigate all of the information you can, in printed text as well as on the Internet.

# Discover True Freedom

Why do I prefer to stitch on my regular machine? Doesn't the size of the machine inhibit the size of my work? How do you get such tiny stitches? I get asked these questions all the time, and I understand them because I was there asking the same things before I learned this skill.

With my home machines, new or old, I can use the smallest darning foot to stitch in any direction, allowing me to follow the outline of anything I can draw. I learned to free-motion quilt without a stitch regulator, so for me, using one would be like adding training wheels to a bike you have ridden for five years.

I don't use a frame to hold the fabric or a carrier to move the machine either. Each of these devices invented to make the job easier feel like governors on an engine, inhibiting my performance. While I have learned to use them, and encourage you to use them if you feel they benefit your work, I feel they are barriers to my freedom.

I enjoy the serenity of just me and my machine, with the fabric all puddled around me. I am not limited to traveling in a section of the quilt, nor restricted to lanes of space. No gadgets, gloves, or fabric movers—free motion is, for me, freeing.

With this style of work, I love what I do. When I learned to free-motion quilt on my home machine, my whole life changed. It has enabled me to stitch anything I have imagined so far and I will always strive to achieve more. I hope you will, too.

# The Checkered Flag

The concepts presented in this book are my way of making sense of this skill. I hope my words and thoughts not only make the job easier for you but also inspire you. Choose today to set a higher standard for yourself and let your quilting be a source of fulfillment in your life. And when you make a quilt for someone special, be sure to add the label.

"Fais de beaux reves" - "Sweet Dreams"
Joanie Zeier Poole
5193 Nelson Rd.
Sun Prairie, WI
608-837-3282

**Project:**

# Quilted Neck-Roll Pillow

This lovely neck-roll pillow will add elegance to any room, and it's quick and easy to sew. The pillow cover is designed to fit a manufactured pillow form, purchased at your local fabric store, or you can make your own. The quilting designs can be easily printed from the CD included in the back of the book.

## Materials

Solid color top fabric ¾ yard
    18" x 22" for top
    2 pieces 5½" x 20" for end panels
Batting 18" x 22"
Lining 18" x 22"

## Supplies

Water-soluble marker
Sewing machine with darning foot
Pillow form 6" x 14"
Lightweight thread to match top
    fabric
Scraps of fusible web
1⅔ yards of ½" wide ribbon

## Cutting

### Quilted panel

Top fabric 18" x 22"
Batting 18" x 22"
Lining fabric 18" x 22"

### End panels

Cut two pieces size 5½" x 20"

# Preparing to Quilt

*1* Print all four sections of the pillow quilting pattern from the CD.

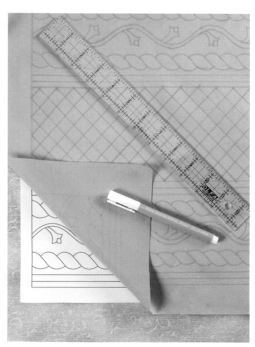

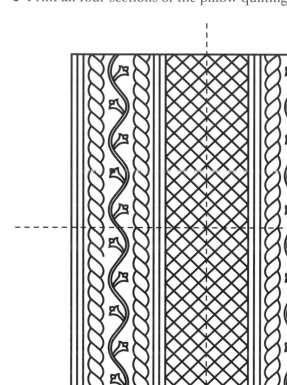

*2* Tape the pattern sections together, trimming off the extra white space as needed.

*3* Tape the assembled pattern to a table, or a light box if necessary.

*4* To mark the center of the top fabric, fold it in half lengthwise and crosswise then crease the folds in the center.

*5* Place the top fabric over the pattern, aligning their centers, and tape the fabric to the table.

*6* Trace the quilting pattern on the top fabric with a water-soluble marker. Use a ruler to keep the straight lines neat.

*7* Layer the lining fabric, batting, and top fabric and pin-baste the layers.

# Quilting the Panel

Use the lightweight thread to quilt the design, following this sequence:

*1* Stitch the straight channels first to anchor the layers.

*2* Add the grid, referring to the information on stitching grids in Step Six.

*3* Stitch the vines and rope designs. Check Step Three for some help with these.

*4* Fill in the background around the motifs with stippling. Remember that it should touch the edges of the lines and motifs.

*5* Remove the marker with cold water and lay the piece flat to dry.

*6* Trim the edges of the panel to ½" past the quilted lines. The panel will be 15" x 20".

# Preparing the End Pieces

*1* Hem the short sides of one end piece by pressing them over ¼" and ¼" again. Fuse or stitch the fold.

*2* Press one long edge over ¼", and again ¼", then press. Fold over 1" along that same edge. The resulting rectangle will be 3½" wide.

*3* Open the fold and lay a 30" piece of ribbon along the fold.

*4* Sew along the fold to form casing. Avoid catching the ribbon in the stitching.

*5* Repeat steps 1 through 4 for the other end piece.

*"It's not how much we give but how much love we put into giving."* Mother Teresa

## Pillow Assembly

*1* Center one end panel on each long side of the quilted panel and pin, matching raw edges.

*2* Using ½" seam allowances, sew the end pieces to the panel, securing the ends with a few backstitches. (Sew with the quilted panel on top so you can use the outer quilted line as your stitching guide.)

*3* Sew the raw ends of the quilted panel together, forming a tube.

*4* Turn the pillow cover right side out and pull the pillow form into the cover. Tighten the ribbons and tie them in nice bows. Hand-stitch the opening closed, if desired.

## Making a Pillow Form

You can purchase a pillow form or use the following instructions to make your own.

### Supplies

½ yard of muslin

### Bag of polyester filling

1 Cut two muslin circles 6½"

2 Cut one muslin rectangle 15" x 19"

3 Using ½" seam allowances, stitch the 15" ends of the rectangle together, leaving a 5" opening at the center for turning and stuffing.

4 Sew a circle to each 19" side of the rectangle.

5 Turn the pillow form right side out and stuff it with polyester filling and sew the opening closed.

# Joanie's
# Quilting Elements
# *Gallery*

All artwork in this gallery is the original work of the author.

Ivy Curl Quilt, 2007

Love Pillow from Fancy Alphabet Pattern, 2002

Huron Quilts, 2007, printable designs on CD.

Floral Heart Wreaths, 2007, from Prairie Rose Pattern

Shadow appliqué pillow, 2003

Geneva Quilt, 2007, Options Stencil from Golden Threads

These simple table pads are machine quilted.

Machine-quilted checkerboard

Heart's Desire Pillow from *Elegant Machine Quilting* and *Ivy Wreath Quilt*

Delectable Mountain Quilt, 1997, by author, Hand Hooked Rug by Margaret Walsh Zeier

Single Initial Pincushion from Fancy Alphabet Pattern and Tablemat from Ivy Wreath Pattern

Radiant Elements Quilt, 2007, Radiance fabric by Robert Kaufman. Elements Stencil Packets from Golden Threads.

Neck-roll Pillow and Strippy Quilt. Printable design on the CD.

Emma Wholecloth Tablemat, Elements Stencil Packet from Golden Threads

# Glossary

**Continuous line designs** Quilting pattern stitched with an uninterrupted line of thread.

**Continuous object designs** Connected rows of stylized quilting motifs stitched with a continuous line of thread.

**Continuous outline designs** Quilting patterns consisting of a puffy channel of space, with or witout motifs attached, stitched with a continuous line of thread.

**Domestic or Home sewing machine** A regular sewing machine.

**Fill patterns** Repeated patterns used to fill background space.

**Feed dogs** Metal teeth under the stitch plate that move the fabric as you sew.

**Free-motion quilting** Lines of stitching sewn on a sewing machine, with a darning foot attached and feed dogs lowered.

**Jump stitch** A way to travel from one motif to another by dragging the thread.

**Layout** The quilt composition. A plan for the placement of blocks, borders, and quilting designs.

**Locking stitches** Securing the thread at the beginning and end of a line of stitching.

**Long-arm** A large quilting machine head mounted on a rack that moves across a quilt attached to rollers.

**Meandering** A larger version of stippling.

**Motif** An individual quilting design.

**Navigation** The driving plan for each design.

**Retrace** Sewing the same line of stitching more than once.

**Seam line** A line of stitching that holds the patchwork and borders together.

**Stippling** A curving, continual line of stitching that fills the background around quilted motifs.

**Stitch in the ditch** Quilting directly in the seam lines, which holds the layers together.

**Stitchable design** A phrase I coined for image outlines that are simple enough to follow with a line of stitching.

**Walking foot** A foot attachment that works with the feed dogs to move the layers of fabric evenly while you sew.

# Resources

I would like to thank the following companies for their generous educational support and for providing supplies for the completion of the projects in this book:

**American Folk and Fabric, Inc.**
*Wonderful, historically based fabric*
www.americanfolkandfabric.com

**Famore Cutlery** (Mr. Scissors)
*Scissors and snips*
www.famorecutlery.com

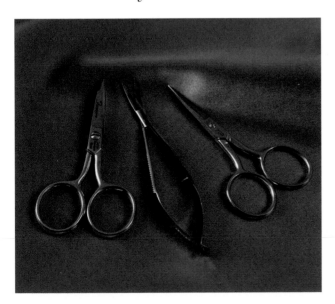

Snips **Free-Motion Slider™**
*Supreme Slider™*
*Magic Bobbin Washers*
www.freemotionslider.com

Magic Bobbin washers control bobbin spin at high speeds

Joanie's designs, Elements Stencil Packets,
and Options Interchangeable Stencils

## Golden Threads
*Marking supplies and stencils*
www.goldenthreads.com

## Harriet's Treadle Arts
*Grid Marker by the Stencil Company*
www.harriethargrave.com

## Heirloom Quilting Designs
*Joanie's quilting products and patterns, award-winning quilts and teaching information*
www.heirloomquiltingdesigns.com
email www.heirloomquilts@hotmail.com

## Hobbs Bonded Fibers
*Heirloom and Tuscany Wool Batting*
www.hobbsbondedfibers.com

## Olfa®
www.olfa.com

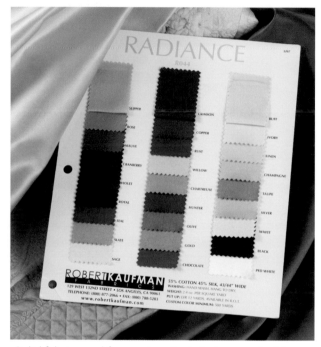

Solid fabric used for most projects is the wonderful new
silk-cotton blend called Radiance.

## Robert Kaufman Fabrics
www.robertkaufman.com

## RJR Fabrics
www.rjrfabrics.com

## Superior Threads
*The Bottom Line thread*
www.superiorthreads.com

## YLI Corporation
*100-weight silk thread*
www.ylicorp.com

# About the Author

The first thing you notice when you look at a quilt made by Joanie Zeier Poole is that the quiltmaker is skillful, sentimental, and unique. She is an artist who has chosen quilting as her medium.

This award-winning quilter has been creating heirloom machine-quilted artwork on a domestic sewing machine for eight years. Her quilts have been exhibited at major quilt shows, making an emotional connection with viewers and earning many awards, including best of show honors at Road to California 2006 and Pacific International Quilt Festival 2006.

Through her business, Heirloom Quilting Designs, Joanie creates original patterns for quilting, appliqué, and embroidery. She uses her imagination, combined with training for her recent degree in graphic design, to offer new products with elegance and sophistication for the quilting community.

Joanie began as a student of master quilter Diane Gaudynski and has taken the craft to a level where she has taught alongside her mentor and other top instructors at events like the Harriet Hargrave Machine Quilting Celebration. She brings to the classroom a warm and informative teaching style, conducting workshops on design and heirloom-machine quilting, using home machines.

All of these talents come together in her books. As the artist, she combines her original drawings and ideal fabrics; as the skilled craftswoman, she constructs the project; then styles the beautiful photographs for you to enjoy. As the graphic designer, she also draws the illustrations to support her unique insights for any machine quilter.

Now, with this second book in the Quilters Workshop Series, Joanie invites you into her workshop to share her exciting new concepts for navigating and stitching quilting designs. Expand your quilt planning know-how with *Joanie's Design Elements* and combine that with *Joanie's Quilting Elements*, a new pathway to success for stitching elegant designs.

Visit Joanie's web site at
www.heirloomquiltingdesigns.com and
contact her at heirloomquillts@hotmail.com

## Also Available From Krause Publications

### Elegant Machine Quilting

*Innovative Heirloom Quilting Using any Sewing Machine*
20 patterns for Innovative Heirloom quilting using
any sewing machine, includes full-size patterns.
ISBN 13: 978-0-89349-878-4
ISBN 10: 0-87349-898-4
$24.99 U.S.
#ELMQ

### Joanie's Design Elements

*8 Easy Lessons to Adapt and Use Quilting Designs*
Guidebook for creating perfectly fitting
quilting designs, includes CD of original
quilting designs.
ISBN 13: 978-0-89689-522-5
ISBN 10: 0-89689-522-X
$29.99 U.S.
Z0851

# On the CD

Wide rope, 2"

Classic Tile Square, 4"

Wreath, 10"

Greek Key, 2"

Huron Square, 7"

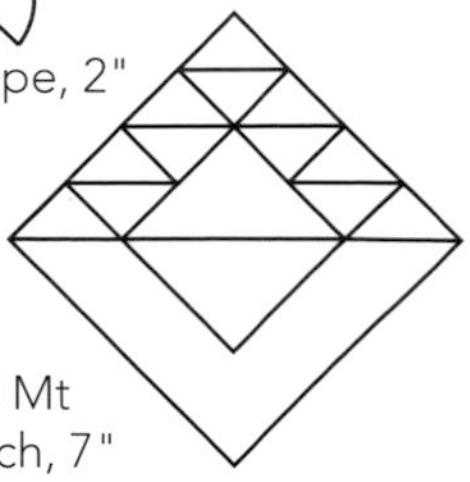

Del Mt Patch, 7"

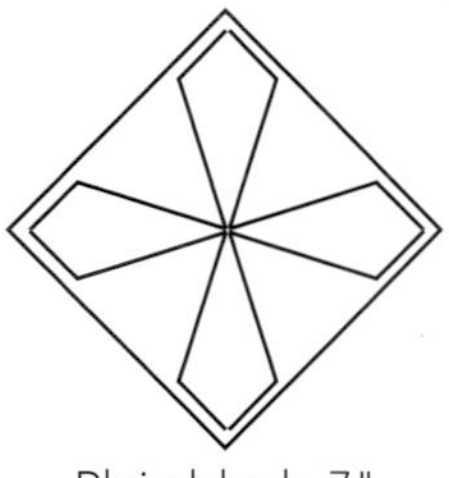

Plain block, 7"

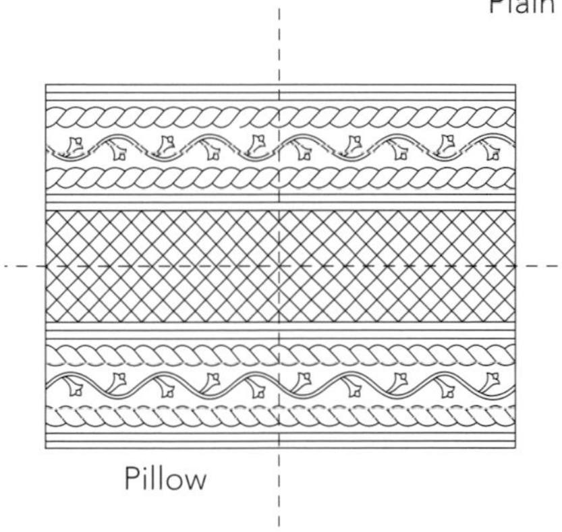

Pillow

Stippling Exercise

Huron 1 - 4"

Huron 2 - 4"

Huron 3 - 5.5"

Huron 4 - 5.5"

Fluer-de-lis, 3"

Vine, 2"

Rope, 1½"

Shamrock, 3"

Huron 5 - 4"

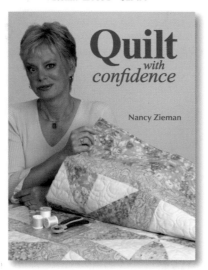
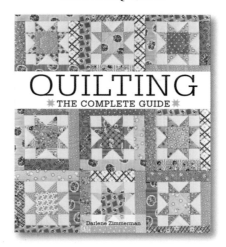